MYCAMINO
WALK#1

20 pilgrims share their insights, their stories and their Camino journey

WRITING MATTERS PUBLISHING

My Camino Walk #1

First published in May 2018

Writing Matters Publishing (UK)
info@writingmatterspublishing.com
www.writingmatterspublishing.com

ISBN 978-1-912774-01-2 (PBK)

Editor: Andrew Priestley

Contributors: Karen Finnin, Jackie Jarvis, Simon Welsh, Sanjiva Wijesinha, Shivantha Wijesinha, Margaret Caffyn, Maeve Samuels, Nathan Fox, Monika Mundell, Dan Stains, Heather Waring, Gabriella Ferenczi, Amanda Candy, Dan Mullins, Anne K Scott, Sarah Hewitt Rippon, Susan Jagannath, Paul Ter Wal, Matt Wright, Janet Russell, Andrew Priestley

This is dedicated to all pilgrims
on the *Camino de Santiago*
and on the *inner journey*
called the *Life Camino.*
Buen Camino!

Contents

Buen Camino!

Dan Mullins
(Radio producer, musician and presenter,
My Camino podcast)

An empty page holds such enormous potential.

I was invited to write the foreword for this compilation of pilgrim stories and I sat with a cup of tea, computer, notebook and ideas.

I host a global podcast called *My Camino* focusing on pilgrims' journeys - a weekly discussion about how the Camino changes lives.

Here, as I write this foreword, the overwhelming feeling is the empty page - the prospect of more, of potential, of growth, of learning, of travel, of seeing and being - is there for all of us.

I look beside the computer at my handwritten notes.

"The Camino de Santiago provides in so many ways ... it enlightens, brightens, shines and guides. It gives us purpose, focus and aim."

I used to be a busy person, a busy soul. The Camino freed me up to be who I hoped I could be, who I should be. I found two gifts - space and time. I hope to make the most of them as time goes on.

My notes say:

"I hope the stories in the following pages give your spirit the energy to find what you're looking for - and you can find in these tales the inspiration to undertake your own pilgrimage. In life and on whatever trail you choose."

Maybe I'm onto something.

Buen Camino ...

The Camino At A Glance

Andrew Priestley

Why would anyone choose to walk hundreds of kilometres over several weeks, when you don't have to?

Why carry a back pack, trudge up and down hills, cross mountains and then endless, featureless country backroads through the sun and the rain, through the heat and the cold? Why endure the exhausting physical and mental challenge of early rising, walking eight to ten hours a day, the blisters, strains and tendonitis; followed by sleepless nights? Why put yourself through all that?

So what exactly is the charm of *El Camino de Santiago (The Way of St James)* in Spain that is luring increasingly more and more people each year from all over the world to do exactly that?

The Camino, historically, was a Holy pilgrimage for Catholics.

We are told that when James the apostle of Christ was martyred in the Holy Land, by Herod in 44AD, his remains were put aboard *a boat made of stone* where it was guided past Gibraltar, and Portugal to an estuary in Galitha (Galicia), Spain to a seaport called Ria Del Rosa Padrone (*pe drone* means big stone).

Story has it that the boat was passing a pagan wedding and the bridegroom was riding a horse along the beach. When he saw the stone boat he became distracted and fell into a wild surf.

As if by miracle both horse and rider were elevated from the churning waves covered in scallop shells - a symbol for rebirth and change (and leaving things behind) - famously depicted in Sandro Botticelli's, *The Birth of Venus* (1485).

The body of St James (San Tiago) was buried in a tomb and over time was lost and forgotten.

The story says, around 813AD, a local shepherd heard voices and was guided by a star to a remote part of a dense wood where he discovered the lost tomb of San Tiago. He promptly informed the local bishop who in turn informed King Alfonso II, The Chaste who made what is now called the first pilgrimage - *the Camino Primitivo.*

At first the tomb was a religious shrine and then a small cathedral was built to house the remains of St James - the Santiago de Compostela.

In 997AD, the shrine and the cathedral were destroyed by the Moorish army and perhaps this became a rallying call to liberate Spain of the Moor invaders.

By the 12th century the cathedral had been rebuilt and pilgrims started to come in earnest. So much so that the *Codex Calixtinus,* a pilgrim's guide setting out the key routes, was written in 1440. It is most likely the world's first tourist guidebook.

And quickly, Santiago became one of the great Catholic pilgrimages alongside the pilgrimage to Jerusalem.

Geoffrey Chaucer's *Canterbury Tales* (1387) is about a group of pilgrims on the *Pilgrims Way* - the UK pilgrimage from Salisbury to Canterbury to visit the tomb of Thomas Becket. But from there, many pilgrims continued onwards to Paris, down through the Dordogne and onto Lourdes and then across the Pyrenees and onwards to the Santiago de Compostela.

And over 1,200 years, literally millions did this pilgrimage.

But from the 16th century onwards, due to church reform and wars, the Camino was inaccessible, or too dangerous and it fell out of favour. And by the 20th century very few even remembered the route.

In 1969, Luis Bunuel released a surrealist film called *The Milky Way* that featured the very strange adventures of two pilgrims on the Camino.

In the 1980s, a Catholic priest, Don Elias Valina Sampedro started to research the original route of the Camino and then introduced the iconic yellow arrows to clearly mark the various pilgimage routes.

Records of pilgrims walking the Camino started to be taken in the late 1980s and in 1987, around 2,900 people registered to walk the Camino.

The Camino was popularised in the book *The Pilgrimage* (1992) by author Paulo Coehlo as his follow up to the best-selling book, *The Alchemist* (1988); by actress Shirley MacLaine in her book *The Camino* (2000), and more recently in the Emilio Estevez film, *The Way* (2010). All reached a massive global audience that has contributed to the Camino growing in both religious and secular popularity.

Subsequently, records show that the numbers of people now walking the Camino has grown exponentially with over 300,000 people in 2017 alone walking from ten official departure points.

Of course, Catholics have continued to walk the Camino as a religious and spiritual pilgrimage, throughout.

The peak period for walking the Camino appears to be between late March and October with the most popular months being July, August and September (which probably coincides with late summer holidays in the northern hemisphere).

The most comfortable months to walk the Camino appear to be Spring (March -May) and Autumn (August-September).

Statistics (2017) show that 27% of pilgrims are aged under 30 years of age, 55% are between 30-60, and 17% are 60+.

The most popular routes are *The French Camino* (63%); *The Camino Portugues* (18%), with the *Camino del Norte, Camino Primitivo, Camino Ingles* and *Via de la Plata* all less than 6%.

Over 25% of pilgrims start from Sarria, located 100kms from Santiago; and 12% start from St Jean Pied de Port in France located over 800 kilometres away.

The UNESCO-listed pilgrimage, *Camino Francés* is still a significant religious walk with a high percentage of Catholic pilgrims; and it is now considered one of the world's great walks along with the *Inca Trail, The Kokoda Trail* and the *88 Temples* in Japan.

In addition to film and literature, the Camino has become the focus of many anthropological studies.

Alex Norman (2009), in explaining why people walk the vast distance of the *Camino Francés*, suggests that distinct from a passive sight-seeing, adventure tour or a consumptive consumer experience, the Camino offers a physical and metaphorical challenge, a journey of meaning and purpose and a lasting sense of achievement. However, he cautions pilgrims against expecting a mystical and magical experience, popularised by Coehlo and MacLaine.

Nancy Frey (2017) suggests that the Camino has historically offered the pilgrim an unique opportunity for introspection and reflection. Her studies are exploring the impact of technology on the Camino experience.

She suggests that you risk losing the essence of that deeply personal introspective journey if you stay connected to the outer world via your mobile phone. The walk instead becomes an exercise in sharing the outer physical experience to an audience via the internet, Tweets, blogs and messaging. While apps can support and guide pilgrims, the pressure to stay connected to the outer world dramatically reduces the inner *Camino experience,* potentially relegating it to a disappointing, arduous and overly long walk.

Articles suggest that merely walking the last 100kms from Sarria, or riding buses through the long boring bits, also deprives the pilgrim of that invaluable inner journey.

The Camino can then easily become a superficial *tick-the-box,* bragging rights exercise.

Dan Mullins, the producer and presenter of the popular weekly podcast *My Camino*, talks about the *rhythm* of the Camino, that only comes from doing the Camino in full.

The majority of pilgrims researched for this book talk about the gains in life perspective that comes from the introspection provided by a very long walk!

My Camino Walk #1 collates the stories of 20 pilgrims - 20 wonderful stories. It provides a marvelous cross-section of experiences that includes the wondrous, the good, the bad and the ugly.

It features pilgrims of all ages - but all young in spirit - walking for a broad and diverse range of reasons.

We have people who walked alone, as couples and in groups. People who walked for hurts or pains, for health or simply for a challenge. We have pilgrims that started from different points and even a pilgrim who walked the Camino in reverse! And pilgrims who met their life partner, and even themselves somewhere on the Camino.

In any case, 20 pilgrims share their stories, their adventures, their journeys, their insights, their practical and emotional walking tips … but ultimately their inspiration.

If you are looking for inspiration you will find it here.

Enjoy. Be inspired.

Buen Camino!

References

- https://en.wikipedia.org/wiki/The_Milky_Way_(1969_film)
- www.caminoways.com
- https://santiagoways.com
- https://www.macsadventure.com/camino-tours/
- https://openjournals.library.sydney.edu.au/index.php/LA/article/view/5001
- https://www.walkingtopresence.com/home/
- https://www.okujapan.com/trips/shikoku-88-pilgrimage-self-guided-4-days-67

A Physiotherapist's Perspective of the Camino de Santiago

Karen Finnin

No doubt many tales of the Camino speak of transformation and rebirth. Mine does not. It still remains, however, one of my proudest life achievements.

If you are lucky enough to have revelation strike you on the trail, embrace it, but don't waste your walk hunting for your lightning bolt. Perhaps all you need, in order to find out who you really are, is a month of fresh air and exercise, void of phone calls, emails, chores and bills.

My name is Karen Finnin. I am an Australian Physiotherapist, and I walked the Camino de Santiago from St Jean Pied de Port to Santiago de Compostela. It was July/August, and took 33 days. I was 31.

On the trail, you will experience peace and beauty, but you may also experience boredom, and you will likely experience pain. If you start the Camino unprepared you will hurt. A lot. Your experience will be compromised, you may not be able to finish, and you could even end up in hospital.

If you think you're pretty fit - perhaps you have run a marathon or two - think again. Camino fitness is a different kind of fitness altogether. Just ask my husband, who had been training with elite level triathletes prior to joining me on the Camino. He crumbled, with gaping red, raw heels by the end of Day 2 on the trail.

On the other hand, give any human six months to adequately prepare for the Camino, and they will gaze up at the Santiago Cathedral with a sense of immense achievement. It will be a walk completed with pride, positivity and a relatively low level of pain.

I am not religious, although I have great respect for the history of the Camino. I walked as a physical challenge, as a pathway to experience a new country, and as a way to strip back the stresses of everyday life. I started alone, and my husband joined me for the final ten days, following a work commitment.

Being a physiotherapist, my curiosity of the Camino revolved around witnessing the capacity of the human body. I saw, and ended up treating, many different ailments that walkers experienced on the trail.

My goal in sharing my tale is to give you some tips to ensure that you start your walk with the best chance of finishing.

Camino favours the prepared over the fit.

I kept a diary on the trail, and wrote in it every day. I'd like to share with you some of these raw thoughts from the trail, followed by a handful of my learnings. Perhaps you will find them helpful.

I have broken my Camino experience up into five stages:

- Days 1-7 Excitement
- Days 8-12 Adaptation
- Days 13-19 Boredom
- Days 20-32 Enjoyment
- Day 33 Euphoria

STAGE 1 - EXCITEMENT

Day 1 - St Jean Pied de Port to Roncesvalles, 24.8 kms. I was the first Pilgrim to arrive at Roncesvalles today. I was very proud!

It was a tough hike, but I made it tougher by barely stopping! I can see that will be my approach – start at 6am and finish by lunchtime, snack while walking, then eat lunch when I arrive. The day is cooler then, and the albergue beds available.

Lessons learned:

At 5 foot 1 and of average fitness, I was far from big, muscular or powerful. Thankfully, preparation turned out to be my super-power. This is what made my first day on the trail so enjoyable.

Immediately prior to starting the Camino, I had completed a 10-day hike in Europe. Prior to that, I had been doing 3-4 hour hikes on weekends. I had built this hiking up over 4-6 months. My pack was a light 10kg, and I had been wearing my loaded pack over the last few months of training before I left Australia.

Roncesvalles is the first stop on the trail for many Camino St James walkers, and it's a tough mountain pass. I observed the other walkers arriving that day. It made me incredibly sad that only one day in, many of the walkers arrived limping, wincing and completely exhausted.

STAGE 2 - ADAPTATION

Day 8 – Legrono to Najera, 29.4 kms. Today was a tough day for me. I didn't sleep well last night (hot and noisy) so was tired and legs aching, balls of feet sore. Water leaked from backpack in morning so I had to fix it.

Started treating some friends: [I list their names and ailments, including calf strain, ankle tendon issue, low back pain, sore ankle, sore feet.]

Bought some sponge at the shop and spent ages making all sorts of supports and cushions for people. Amazingly most had immediate success. That made me very happy.

Lessons learned:

Between Days 7 and 10, my legs ached. I didn't have any blisters, and I couldn't diagnose any particular injury, I just ached from the knees down. In hindsight I can see it was my soft tissues adapting to the increased repetitive load. At the time I thought this ache would remain for the rest of the Camino, bad enough to keep me awake at night. Like magic, however, it suddenly cleared by Day 10.

This was also the time period when my fellow walkers started developing injuries. They had all resulted from unaccustomed load, accumulating over multiple days.

People think it is a lack of cardiovascular fitness that will hold them back on the trail. It is not. For the majority of walkers who experienced issues on the trail, it was tissue tolerance, and not lung capacity, that had unraveled them.

Tissue tolerance is built through a gradual progression of walking volume. Too much too soon and your skin, muscles, bones, tendons and/or joints will break down. Gradual increase over time, and your body will build resilience.

Do the miles, carry the weight, wear your shoes. All well before you hit the trail.

STAGE 3 - BOREDOM

Day 14 – Hontanas to Boadilla, 28.2 kms. When I was walking I was bored again today. The scenery on the Camino is not as beautiful as I thought it would be. There are often trucks and cars and many other Pilgrims on foot and on bikes. We'll see what I think closer to the end.

Lessons learned:

I didn't expect this. I don't know why the boredom surprised me, but it did. After riding the waves of the *Excitement Stage,* and the *Adaptation Stage,* I think my brain just hit a chemical let down. It lasted about a week, before my mindset inexplicably swung into pure happiness, comfort and enjoyment.

STAGE 4 - ENJOYMENT

Day 25 – Ponferrada to Villafranca, 24 kms. Today started with quite heavy rain, so the full wet weather gear was out. The big japara looks stupid, but gee was it worth it today. Between it, the overpants and pack cover, I was dry all day.

Dan is having trouble with pressure points on his feet from his shoes. It's funny, he has more fitness than all of us, but the Camino is more about preparedness and he was not, bless his heart.

Lessons learned:

My husband Dan is fit, super fit. He thrashes me at every athletic endeavour we tackle. Prior to me starting the Camino, we planned for him to join me for the last 10 days, once he completed a work assignment. We pictured that I would be exhausted, and that he would help me and support me to get to the end.

Dan didn't train specifically for the Camino, but had been doing a lot of running, swimming and cycling. He arrived on the trail in running shoes, and was carrying a mammoth 20kg pack.

After two days walking at my pace, his heels were shredded red raw. On his third day he had to get his pack transported so that he didn't have to carry it.

On his fourth day he sticky taped his thongs (flip flops) to his feet, so that the broken skin on his heels could recover while he walked. Hilarious.

Needless to say, the *carer* role was reversed from what we expected!

Day 27 – O Cebriero to Triacastella, 21 kms. Today was foggy all day and damp, but the walk was short – 21 kms. Was glad that Dan did well today with his scuffs taped to his feet.

I heard from Marco* that Luca* went home unwell, ended up in hospital with an infection from the blisters and now has to have some dead muscle surgically removed from his foot! I can't believe it.

Lessons learned:

Footwear and blisters: The worst blisters I saw were on an Italian chap named Luca*. They started on day one, and continued to worsen throughout the hike. He was wearing ankle high hiking boots that he had not broken in enough before he started. As the Camino progressed, several of the blisters had become infected. He eventually had to leave the trail before completion, collapsed at the airport on his way home, and ended up in hospital. The infected blisters were so bad that they had to do surgery on his feet.

I wore hiking shoes, rather than ankle boots on the Camino. From a physio perspective, this is what I recommend. Most of the trail is on flat paths.

As you walk, your ankle naturally moves. Having extra resistance from a boot around your ankle makes the muscles in your calf and shin have to work harder to move. This can lead to overload and injury. Unless you have a known history of ankle instability, shoes are a better choice to decrease the workload of your lower legs on the trail.

Hiking shoes are better than runners, as the durability is far superior. Waterproof hiking shoes are even better.

Ideally your Camino shoes should be worn on all of your training hikes for at least three months before you start. This is my best blister prevention advice.

My second best advice for blisters is intervene as soon as you feel a spot of rubbing develop, before the skin breaks. Cover the area with a breathable tape (e.g. *Fixomull, Hypafix*).

If a blister does develop, *do not,* for crying out loud, use a needle to put a thread through it. I saw so many people do this on the trail, including Luca*. It is a great way to introduce infection. Just protect the area, keep it clean, and let your body do it's thing.

Believe it or not, I didn't get a single blister on the trail, so it is possible. My toes rubbed together sometimes, but *Fixomull* soon took care of it.

Names have been changed.

STAGE 5 - EUPHORIA

Day 33 – Arca do Pino to Santiago de Compostela, 20 kms. Euphoric day! Santiago Cathedral was not a disappointment at all. Saw a lot of familiar faces. Ended up at a little Spanish bar drinking Sangria – perfect!

Lessons Learned:

John Brierley wrote the Camino guidebook that was my constant companion on the trail.

I believe that the Camino strips you back to who you truly are, and John himself described this phenomenon the best:

"Within the crucible that is pilgrimage, a remarkable alchemical reaction takes place that burns away the dross we have collected in our lives, so that, in due course, only the purest gold will remain."

About Karen Finnin

Karen Finnin is a physiotherapist from Melbourne, Australia. After completing the Camino, Karen moved to East Timor due to her husband's work. While living in Dili, Karen set up a physio practice to service the large expat community of diplomats, workers and volunteers that resided there.

After three years, Karen wondered how her loyal clients could continue to benefit from her physiotherapy guidance when they returned to Australia.

Almost by accident, *Online Physio* was born, and with it an international movement in online healthcare.

Online Physio is a website platform that specialises in providing long distance physiotherapy consultations to people who have trouble accessing traditional care.

Karen's online patients include digital nomads, location independent entrepreneurs, expatriates and world travellers. She is now a digital nomad herself, travelling the world with her laptop by her side.

The infamous story of Dan's Camino blisters and sticky taped scuffs continues to be fondly retold at family BBQs, special occasions, and any other time Dan's high level achievements need to be kept in check.

www.online.physio
https://www.facebook.com/physiosonline/
https://www.instagram.com/karen.finnin/
https://www.linkedin.com/in/karenfinnin/

In Pursuit of Slow … My Camino Story

Jackie Jarvis

It all started back in 2015, just after I had a book published called *Quick Wins in Sales and Marketing*. As a business growth coach, this book had been designed to support my clients and build my credibility. The publishers and I had agreed on the best title, *Quick Wins*, since everybody wants things quickly these days … *Fast* sells! And it did. The only problem was that *quick* wasn't really working for me in my own life.

Too much

I was typical of many independent business women; juggling lots of tasks, trying to fit too much in, pushing for more all the time. I never really took my foot off the accelerator … I couldn't stop. I was afraid to … afraid that if I didn't keep pushing I would lose it all … fall behind, or even worse, fail completely.

I had been repeatedly trying over the years to build a business which could provide some leverage and security above and beyond my one-to-one coaching with clients.

However, I seemed to have a knack of picking the wrong partners and each joint venture I set up failed to materialise despite me working harder and harder each time. I had become exhausted trying so hard to make things work.

My head always seemed so full and I was tired of seeing an endless conveyor belt of tasks stretched out before me. Despite the enjoyment I gained from helping people through my coaching work, it was just becoming too much to continue in the same manner. I was losing my mojo, my passion for what I was doing, and that really worried me. I needed something to change, but I wasn't sure what?

A chance meeting ...

A chance meeting with a colleague, Tim, who had just returned relaxed and refreshed from walking the Camino de Santiago (the full *Camino Francés*) sparked my initial interest. Tim had been so passionate about the experience, and to take time out walking the pathways that had been trod by saints and pilgrims over many centuries intrigued me. I knew that I had been neglecting myself and my spiritual side and needed something like this to reawaken my senses. However, I was scared ... scared to take so much time out of my business ... and could I do it physically, I wondered?

Something needed to change ...

After some intensive research, reading John Brierley's guide book, Paolo Coelho's *The Pilgrimage* and watching the film *The Way*, I made the decision that I was going to walk the *Camino Francés*. I shared my thoughts with my partner Matt and he surprised me by saying that he would also like to do it; he felt in need of some reflection time following a stressful period in his life. As it would take about five weeks in total, we decided to walk the Camino together in two stages; that way, we would be able to fit it around our work commitments.

You need to be prepared to walk a Camino; it can entail walking up to 35 kms per day, over often challenging terrain, with summits of up to 1,800 m. So, we did do a fair amount of training beforehand, but nothing could have prepared me for how hard it was to actually carry my backpack over those kinds of distances.

Overloading ...

I stuffed my backpack full to the brim with everything that I thought I might possibly need. There was my complete make-up bag, some heavy books, gadgets, extra clothes and much more besides.

No matter how much I was warned and told that I needed to travel light, I stubbornly reckoned I could carry everything. However, when I first arrived at Saint- Jean-Pied-de-Port in France and tried to put my fully-laden pack on, I nearly fell backwards, just like Cheryl Strayed in the film *Wild!*

One very hot day, after walking about 20 kms, I started to realise exactly what I was doing to myself. Everything ached; my back, my shoulders, my legs. And I wasn't really enjoying the experience. I wasn't paying attention to my surroundings, I could have been anywhere, all I was able to think about was how hard it was. I was trying to walk with a load so heavy that I found myself struggling to see the beauty of the places I was walking through.

I was carrying too much. I couldn't do this. Then it hit me all of a sudden — this was an exact reflection of my business life back in the UK, where I was overloaded and not enjoying it. All I had done was move myself to a different environment ... nothing had changed ... I had just created another type of overload.

Why do I do this to myself?

I threw my ruck sack to the ground and screamed out in frustration, "Why do I always do this to myself?! Why, Why, Why?!" I just stood there helplessly, and in despair looked upwards to the sky and asked for help. I did not know who I was asking and did not expect to receive an answer.

Then, suddenly, I heard a *Voice* ... I wasn't sure if this *Voice* was coming from inside my head (a thought) or from outside ... all I know was that it did not sound like me at all. This *Voice* was soft and gentle.

It whispered to me, "Have the courage to let go of that which does not serve you.", and repeated this a number of times: "Have the courage to let go of that which does not serve you. Have the courage to let go of that which does not serve you."

I stood transfixed. What did it mean? What was it telling me?

The lesson ...

I needed to offload, to let go of the weight that was suffocating me. I took some items out of my rucksack — in fact everything that was not essential — and gave them to an old man that I met later that evening at the albergue where we were staying. I had freed myself of my unnecessary load and was able to start the process of fully enjoying the Camino experience.

As I walked the many miles that followed, I started to reflect on *The Voice*. What was it? Why that particular message? What did I need to learn from it? I decided to call it *The Voice of Slow*.

I came to realise that *The Voice of Slow* is within all of us, but we don't tend to hear it as we're usually too busy, our heads full of too much internal chatter or noise. I didn't hear my *Voice of Slow* fully until I started walking the Caminos.

Let go

I was holding on to things that I really needed to let go of. I had become too accustomed to the load I was carrying. It was only when I realised this, that I was able to do something about it.

We all have things that can hold us back and make our journey through life heavy-going. You sometimes need to go slower to be able to recognise these things, and to realise what may be holding you back. For me, walking the Camino was the experience I needed to reconnect with myself and pay attention to my inner voice.

Still and simple

Slowing down on the Camino had given me a taste of what it can be like when you allow yourself to live life simply, when you slow everything down. It was like going back to being like a native in many respects, moving from place to place every day.

The physical challenge

It is important to look after yourself to be able to walk the distances you set for yourself each day. Do take a sun hat or a cap, twice on the route for various reasons I found myself without one and had to resort to using branches of a tree tucked inside a headband to fend off the sun. The only problem was it made it much harder to see the signs!

Listen to your body and pay attention to what it is telling you it needs.

I always remember an older lady, Alice, I kept coming across, who didn't look like she could walk very far at all. One day when I asked her what her plans were she just said, 'My body lets me know how far I can go ... I have time ...' A lovely example of someone who was obviously listening to her own *Voice of Slow* whilst still challenging herself physically.

Having now walked over 1,250 miles of various Camino routes to Santiago (the *Francés, Portuguese,* and *del Norte* routes), my *Voice of Slow* has given me many insights and reflections which have inspired me. I have shared these in my book, *In Pursuit of Slow.*

UK *https://www.amazon.co.uk/dp/B0731QN87L*
USA *https://www.amazon.com/gp/aw/d/B0731QN87L*

The challenge for me was to bring back the Camino lessons and apply them to normal everyday life. Life that brings with it a very different set of pressures and stresses.

People often ask me how my life has changed and how do I maintain the lessons learnt walking the Camino?

Well, it's not quite that simple and I am definitely still a work in progress! I did find that walking the Camino and writing my book gave me the courage to let go of many of the things that were not serving me in my life. I asked for help and I received it. It hasn't been easy or straightforward, but no real growth ever is, is it? I find it easier to maintain a healthy balance by fitting in walking, running, yoga, and meditation into my daily life, which also helps to manage stressful times and maintain my energy and vitality. I will continue to do an annual pilgrimage, as I now see it as a vital part of my life.

How to hear your *Voice of Slow* whilst walking the Camino:

- **Travel light.** Weigh everything and only take what is essential. The lighter your load, the greater freedom you will feel.

- **Focus on the NOW.** Just switch off to everything except what you are doing every day, every moment. Notice and be grateful for simple pleasures. You will start to feel a growing sense of wellbeing with each day that passes.

- **Give yourself silent time.** Walk without talking for periods of time. Take time alone for refection.
Allow yourself some mental space and relaxation.

- **Capture your reflections each day in a journal or blog.** Don't judge, just write what comes naturally, it may surprise you. Get to know yourself through your walking.
- **Go at your own pace.** This is not a race to the finish line, it is a journey to your own destination. You are not in competition with anyone. Look after your body and take regular breaks when you need it.
- **Trust that you will always find your way.** There are always signs to follow and people to help. The Camino will look after you.
- **Pay attention and you will learn what you need to.** This is part of it. Be observant.
- **Start to notice and enjoy the peace.** It is from this peace that your greatest feelings of joy will come.

I am truly grateful for my experiences walking the Camino Routes, to all the people I met on my travels and to Matt with whom I walked the Frances Route in 2015, The Portuguese Route in 2016 and the first half of the Norte Route in 2017. Our daily blog shares our wonderful experiences with humour, insight, as well as the practicalities.

Find it at *www.jackiemattadventures.com*

I will also continue to share insights and lessons from future Camino walking and *The Voice of Slow* in my *In Pursuit of Slow Community www.FB.com/inpursuitofslow* and blogs on *www.inpursuitofslow.com*

Enjoy!

About Jackie Jarvis

Jackie is a business growth coach and runs mastermind groups. She primarily helps over loaded SME business owners and their teams take regular time out from working in their business, to regain clarity and focus.

She helps create positive momentum by providing the reflection and accountability framework necessary to ensure desired plans and ambitions are fulfilled, as well as, personal wellbeing maintained. *Slowing Down to Gain More* is her mantra.

She is the published author of three books, *85 Inspiring Ways to Market Your Business* (2010), *Quick Wins in Sales and Marketing* (2015) and *In Pursuit of Slow* (2017). She is the creator of *The Client Growth Club* an online membership site for coaches and consultants (2018).

Jackie gives talks on the power of *Slowing Down to Gain More*, sharing lessons learnt whilst walking the Camino de Santiago and how they can be applied in business.

Jackie lives in the historic Oxfordshire market town Wallingford, and in her spare time you may find her walking or running along the Thames Path and Chiltern Way.

https://www.linkedin.com/in/jackie-jarvis-b8727212
www.jackiejarvis.co.uk
www.inpursuitofslow.com
www.FB.com/inpursuitofslow
Twitter @inpursuitofslow and @jackiejarvis1

And So I Walk

Simon Welsh

I had been looking for home since I was a child: Dorothy had been taught by Glinda, the witch of the North, that there was no place like it; a cat and two dogs had risked hell and high water to get there in Disney's *Homeward Bound*. And it was what I ached for every time my primary school teacher would deny me toilet access until she'd made me crap my pants, just so she could humiliate me in front of the entire class and send me, in *shitty-bum-shame*, to the school nurse to be sterilised.

Trauma is a peculiar thing. If it goes unchecked it can manifest much later in life in such abstract ways that, at first glance, they seem totally unrelated to the original incident. But when your parents don't know how to protect you from the school monster, *home* is just a reprieve from Hell and never really feels like a safe place.

It wasn't until I was getting addicted to crystal meth and sex parties in central London, some 30 years later that I realised I was *still* looking for home. Except, now, I was looking in some of the darkest spaces the cultured world had to offer. Looking back I guess that I'd given up ever really finding such a place. After all, it was probably somewhere over the rainbow.

And here I was, 36 years old, walking step-by-step to Finisterre; literally, the end of the world. Maybe I would find the rainbow there.

It was Day 24 of a 40-day Camino. I was averaging about 30 kms a day.

And I was in a state of deep and humble surrender, having given up sex, porn, Tina, cigarettes, coffee, bread, meat, fish, eggs and dairy: *abstinence* and *veganism* are not two words I would usually be associated with, but these were desperate times.

Judith, Erik, Alessandro and I had stayed in a monastery the night before. Apart from the two German ladies who had tried to take over the place by covert invasion, there had been little to no incident.

We had agreed where we would all end up that evening, which allowed us the freedom to walk at our own pace. And it meant that I could spend a lot of the day walking alone along a road that filled me with excitement . . .

Long and straight, it stretched out in front of me as far as the eye could see.

By early evening I had climbed the best part of all the stairs in World Trade Centres 1 and 2 (before their tragic and suspicious demise) and could look back down across the 18 kms I'd walked that day. My feet were glowing in my shoes; almost throbbing, as if they each had their own heart.

Several times already I had mistaken a turn in the path for an indication that the climb was over, only to find another longer, steeper, muddier challenge than the one I'd just completed. So when the mud gave way to tarmac and I saw three small buildings on the left and five on the right, I almost sailed right through, believing my destination to be at least another 2 kms further up the road.

There was a little bench outside a closed door. And with only 2 kms left to walk I almost didn't stop. But my backpack wasn't sitting right and the left strap was starting to dig into my shoulder. So I sat down and unclipped my pack at the waist and the chest, marvelling at the delicious feeling of being released from something heavy. The only feeling I've ever had that is comparable is the feeling I get when I turn off an extraction fan that has been running in the background for a long time, or perhaps a really slow long wee, sitting down. It's like silence with sprinkles.

The sun was setting like red liquid being poured down the back of the far hills, and I was enjoying this sacred wonder in the blissful feeling that I was now 10 kilos lighter. I was almost in tears I was so happy: I had climbed to the top of a mountain today. And now I was being given a little piece of heaven, just because I happened to be sitting on this particular bench at this particular moment.

Could life get any better?

"Ha-lo," came a soft gravelly voice. I turned my head slowly to see a beautiful bearded, gentle faced, sparkling-eyed man standing in the doorway.

"Ju-won-to estey heer? Pliz. Follow me."

And then he disappeared into the doorway. I thought he must be an angel. Maybe I was dead and this was actually heaven.

Yes. Apparently life could, indeed, get better

I got up, slung my pack over one shoulder and followed the angel into a small stone floored anti-room that was clearly just for shoes and coats.

"Pliz," said the angel smiling at me, *"take off jour choose. Ju-R home now. Yes? My name is Alejandro."* (Of course it was.) *"Wot iz jour nayme pliz?"*

"Simon," I croaked. I was suddenly exhausted and felt like I wanted to cry. I wasn't sure quite why but it felt good. I carried on unlacing my shoes and my tight feet breathed a sigh of relief.

"My home is jour home. Dinner is at eight. Give me your clothes. I wash. I dry. I give back."

This all sounded wonderful but my budget would probably not stretch to such luxuries.

"How much?" I asked.

"Ju decide how much iz for ju. For dinner; washing; drying; food, joz pute in box when ju leev. This is the 'donativo' way." I would learn later what that meant.

Erik, Alessandro and Judith arrived not long after and were all greeted with the exact same magical introduction from

35

Alejandro, who was clearly working in service to something bigger than himself, in the amount of heart he put into making conscious connections with all his guests.

Before dinner there was a talk about the choice that lay before us ... the *hospitales* route (the high road) or the low road which would be gentler with more stopping places and an extra albergue, though Alejandro would not tell us where the best albergues were as he said that would make it his Camino rather than ours.

The *hospitales* route sounded very appealing.

At the highest point there were three *hospital* ruins, places where the first pilgrims slept sheltered from the elements. Some died along the way in those harsh times. Alejandro asked us to consider *the way* and to take strength from the millions of footsteps that had trodden the way before us.

"When ju feel ty-red an-ju ask-een 'why ai not at de'home comfortable??' then as ju wal-keen ju muz-tu-sei, 'Thank you, thank you, thank you' with each step. That is 'the way'. And then you learn to make the way in the life like you make in Santiago. This is why I hospitalero: to show 'the way.'"

The four of us sat eating dinner with strangers, and by the time we were tucking into a bowl of lavish fresh fruits on the table, we had all become friends. We had been *Alejandro'd* with a Camino bond that would never be broken. Not that any of us could know that yet.

That night I had a dream I was building a house on the beach. I was doing it all myself. And in the dream I had the skills to make a really excellent job of it. But when I looked out of the upstairs windows my heart was filled with dread at what I saw.

I knew that I was going to have to die to who I thought I was, so that I could be released to be who I really am; like a bird being let out of a cage. But my identity was steeped in who I was. And I wasn't prepared to let go of being that person. Not yet. I was going to have to suffer a lot more before I was prepared to surrender my identity. I would have to go beyond Finisterre, the end of the world. I would have to die.

The Conscious Engineer

I'm a simple builder. I am building all the time.
I built the house I live in and the stairs that let me climb
To the first and second floors that help me see a broader view
Of the world that I inhabit: the world I share with you.

Did you know that you're a builder, building all the time?
It's easier to hear if I tell you in a rhyme,
That everything we do and think; everything we say
Is building our reality, every single day.

And if we understand this, if we really let it sink,
If we know that we are building every time we speak and think;
If we see that every action is a window pane or brick,
Or a flight of stairs, we start to see that building happens quick.

Today I saw the building I've been building for a while,
And though it has a structure and a shape that makes me smile,
It's a building on the sand. I've been building at low tide.
And when the tide comes in again; there's nowhere I can hide.

So I'm opening my backpack, packing only what I need.
The tide will be upon me soon. It's coming in at speed.
I look out to the West where the sky is yellow dark
Above a thrashing sea that's hungry to consume me like a shark.

And then I turn to face the window out towards the East,
Where I know that, in a moment, Dawn will start to be released.
I cannot see the sunlight yet. Dawn has not arrived.
But every journey starts in darkness; that's how we've survived.

Through a hundred thousand years of our journey on the Earth,
Trying to understand exactly how much we are worth.
And the journey starts in faith. For, in the dark, we cannot see
How invaluable and precious our potential aches to be.

So once again, I have to leave behind what I have built:
A house with a foundation made of mortar mixed with guilt.
I do not want to leave – I've been building this for years –
I've toiled hard and built this place through blood and sweat
and tears.

But the path is calling out to me to walk towards the East;
The tide is coming in like a ruthless savage beast.
The sea will soon consume this house. It's time for me to leave,
On the path towards a sunrise that I'm ready to receive.

Walking the Camino changed my life. Did it cure me? No. I will always be an addict. Something like that must never be painted over for fear of a relapse.

But something began to shift in me on that adventure. And now, though I am far from *healed* (whatever that means), sometimes when I walk somewhere, even to the shops, I feel Alejandro's words rumbling in my heart like the wisdom of Old Father Time:

"When ju feel ty-red an-ju ask-een 'why ai not at de'home comfortable??' then as ju wal-keen ju muz-tu-sei, 'Thank you, thank you, thank you' with each step. That is 'the way'. And then you learn to make the way in the life like you make in Santiago."

So, to you that have now come to the end of my story, I say, "Thank you. Thank you. Thank you."

About Simon Welsh

Simon Welsh' poetry spans many concepts, from the magical and ridiculous, through the harsh stark truth behind 21st century society, to practical solutions to leading a whole and happy life.

Essentially there is a single message running through the work: we are all connected.

The power of the Universe runs through us. In some this power is active and in others, dormant: every piece of work is an invitation to step out of dormancy and into activity, where we can dance our own unique dance with pride and with joy, and shift into the understanding of what it truly means to be our own hero and to live in love rather than fear.

We can make every day count by choosing, moment by moment, to realise our dreams and our fantasies, pulling them out of imagination and creating them in reality. Thus we can share with the world the gifts we brought to the Earth. It is time to remember how powerful we are, and to give to the world what we want the world to give to us: Appreciation, compassion, forgiveness, humility, understanding and valor.

Simon's journeys have taken him to the heights of wonder, and the depths of despair. He has done battle with Goblins and other dark forces. He has met gnomes, faeries and angels, and has often found himself living a life that feels more like it comes from a story than something that is actually happening in *real life.*

But if we are honest, do any of us know what that is any more?

www.simonwelshpoetry.co.uk
www.twitter.com/simonthepoet
www.facebook.com/simonthepoet

Dinner by Candlelight

Sanjiva Wijesinha and Shivantha Wijesinha

The picturesque little town of St Jean Pied de Port – very small, very French – lies nestled in the foothills of the Pyrenees.

It was from here, way back in April 2011 that the two of us – Sanjiva and Shivantha, father and son, pilgrims in a strange land and strangers in Spain - began our Camino.

From the welcoming pilgrim office in St Jean we were able to get ourselves pilgrim passports called *Credencials* – documents which entitled us to obtain overnight accommodation in the many specially set up pilgrim refuges, called *albergues,* along the Camino.

Maintained by municipalities, church organizations, monasteries or private individuals, these albergues (also known as *aubergues* or *refugios*) are found, generally no further than ten to 15 kilometres apart, in most of the small towns and villages through which the Camino passes. They provide a cheap place to stay for the night. This is often in the form very basic accommodation, just bunk beds in dormitories – but with clean (usually) sheets, at €5-10 for the night, who will complain?

During our six-week journey along the 800 kms plus *Camino Francés* we stayed in various types of accommodation – some comfortable and others not so – but our serendipitous stay at the albergue of San Nicolas in Puente Itero was certainly one of the most memorable.

I feel that serendipity was responsible for our stay at this particular albergue because it came about quite unexpectedly as a result of Shivantha (who speaks fluent Italian) falling into conversation the previous evening with an Italian pilgrim from Trento in Italy. It was Ruggero who told Shivantha about San Nicolas – and so we resolved to make that our next destination.

This little albergue, manned by three to four *hospitaleros*, is situated near the bridge of Puente Itero in an ancient building which was recently restored by the Perrugia-based Confraternity of St James (*Confraternita di San Jacopo di Compostella*). Located where a 12th century pilgrim hospice once stood, it consists of a single long hall with a small chapel at one end and a set of five double-bunk beds at the other end – with a long dining table in the middle.

What was so special about this albergue was not its location nor even its atmosphere of antiquity - but the exemplary spirit of service shown by the *hospitaleros*. All the other places at which we stayed during our Camino were essentially run as commercial establishments, providing cheap accommodation and food for pilgrims journeying along the Way, but in a manner and at a price designed to earn a living for those running these establishments.

San Nicolas, however, was different. Here we did not have to pay a fee on arrival. We were welcomed, and when we asked about payment we were told that we could make a donation (*donativo*) when we left the following morning.

The albergue itself had no electricity. Lighting was provided entirely by candles and cooking was done on a gas stove. Behind the main albergue was a garden in which there was a small building (which fortunately had electric lights and hot water!) that housed toilets and showers. There was also a quaint hand operated pump nearby that enabled water to be drawn from the well so one could wash one's clothes.

The *hospitaleros* provided pilgrims with a cooked dinner. We were treated to salad, pasta, chorizo and cake, but before dinner, we were privileged to participate in a ceremony, unique among all the albergues in which we stayed – and one which epitomised the humility and sense of dedication which these *hospitaleros* brought to their task of caring for pilgrims.

At 7.30 in the evening, all 12 pilgrims staying at the

albergue were asked to be seated in a semicircle in the chapel. The *hosplitaleros* were all wearing magnificent black capes embroidered with scallop shells.

One by one we submitted ourselves to the ceremony.

Each of us was asked in turn to place one foot in a bowl held by one of them – and while another *hospitalero* read a prayer of blessing, a third poured water from a special pitcher on to our feet and washed it. After drying the foot with a towel, the *hospitalero* who had washed the foot kissed it. This was certainly a demonstration of the true humility (reminding all of us about Christ washing his disciples' feet before the *Last Supper*) with which these special men accepted their calling.

Following the ceremony of having our feet washed, we were asked to sit down at the long table and served dinner. The only light was provided by long candles placed along the centre of the table and in a few strategically placed holders along the walls. Our offers to help with serving and clearing up were gently declined. *"No, Pilgrims, you are tired. You must sit and allow us to serve you".* Making conversation in a mixture of Italian, French, Spanish and English, we felt a genuine sense of fellowship with our fellow pilgrims.

Roland, who had walked all the way from Lyon in France with his pet donkey Praline and was planning to get to Santiago for his 65th birthday on June 10th, was chatting in French with Shivantha - while Ruggero from Trento in Italy, Michelle from Toronto in Canada and Sanjiva from Melbourne in Australia were engaged in a most entertaining trilingual conversation about our work and families back home, making up with hand gestures and body language what our limited knowledge of each other's languages would not allow us to do more accurately!

When dinner was finished we all sat on the wooden benches outside the albergue. The sun was going down and soon the glow of the setting sun caressed the landscape.

In time darkness fell, the moon emerged – and after a while we could see above us a spectacular night sky.

Far from the pollution and smog of the big city, the stars and constellations were so clear. No wonder that this pilgrimage was called *The Way of the Stars!*

It was not difficult to understand how easy it would have been for folk in medieval times to believe that the sky above their heads was a barrier – a semi-permeable membrane if you will – that literally separated us humans down below from God and his people up in heaven.

Given the vista of the sky as we were privileged to witness here, it was not difficult for us to empathise with such a view.

Shivantha and Ruggero had found a guitar somewhere inside the albergue and sang for us as we sat outside – after which each of us was encouraged to sing a song in our own language. A couple of the Dutch ladies even danced to one of Shivantha's songs!

Sharing this experience of pilgrimage so far from home created a unique spirit of conviviality among this group of beings who were outwardly so different yet inwardly so connected.

It was certainly an evening to remember. All of us who came to this place as strangers came to realise that simple yet profound truth: there is much more in this world that we have in common than that which divides us.

We had come to the albergue San Nicolas as individuals journeying along a path of pilgrimage, but we left the next morning as friends – in truth, as members of that great family of pilgrims united by the Camino.

Our experience of walking the Camino could well be summed up in the beautiful words from the Indian poet Rabindranath Tagore's poem Gitanjali:

> *"Thou hast made me known to friends whom I knew not.*
> *Thou hast given me seats in homes not my own.*
> *Thou hast brought the distant near -*
> *and made a brother of the stranger."*

About Dr. Sanjiva Wijesinha

Medical doctor, army officer, university professor, prolific writer and inveterate traveller, Sanjiva is originally from Sri Lanka. Educated in Sri Lanka and Oxford, he now lives in Australia and is a best-selling author (*Friends, Not Our War, Strangers on the Camino, Tales from my Island*).

Sanjiva's illustrated book *Strangers on the Camino* is available in paperback from *Vijitha Yapa Publications, Sri Lanka, Dymocks Bookshops* in Melbourne; and on Amazon at:

http://www.amazon.com/Strangers-Camino-Father-Holy-Trail
-ebook/dp/B00JO1ZC40
https://sanjivawijesinha.wordpress.com/
https://www.facebook.com/Strangersonthecamino/

About Shivantha Wijesinha

Sanjiva's son Shivantha grew up in Oxford, Sri Lanka, Hong Kong and Australia and qualified as a lawyer.

He then studied at *The American Academy of Dramatic Arts* in New York. He is now an actor (*Death Trail* 2018, *City of Mercy* 2017) and musician (*By the Window, Flowers in Her Hand*) living in New York.

https://www.shivantha.com/
Album: *https://www.amazon.com/*
Clarity-Shivantha/dp/B079CSSDX3

Answer When It Calls

Margaret Caffyn

We are all born with innocence and the power to make what we want out of life. Sometimes we lose our way with the responsibilities and expectations put upon us, but if we are lucky enough we wake up one day and realise that there must be more … more fulfilment, more enjoyment, and that is just what happened to me.

I had been swallowed by work, grief, and just life in general, so I got myself a backpack and walked across Spain. What followed was unimaginable and my life changed completely. I struggled over the Pyrenees, floated inside my mind on the Meseta, and washed my soul in the Galician rain. I was bathed, cleansed and humbled by the *Camino Francés*.

What makes a person want to do this?

We have no idea, but it certainly makes you feel alive. Very few people only do a Camino once. We are all filled with the internal longing, an ache, to return to the simplicity and freedom of the Camino.

The following year, I tackled the rugged and less traveled *Via de la Plata*, the old trade route from the south to the north of Spain.

Having done my inner work on the *Camino Francés*, I set out with an open mind, an open heart and no expectations, with a friend I had met on the other Camino. It was really tough, in many different ways.

It is not just a stroll through the countryside with the warm sun slowly tanning your skin and a gentle breeze blowing through your hair.

We struggled with temperatures over 40 degrees in *Extremadura* with no shelter, trees or cafes with red plastic chairs, and found that it was actually quite mountainous as well. We had food poisoning, we were chased by pigs and walked the path of fear through fields of bulls with huge horns and beady eyes. We were confronted by wolves up in the mountains and we waded our way through a swarm of flying ants (of biblical proportions) swatting them frantically from our eyes, hair, mouths and we learned that it is possible to run quite fast with a backpack on!

My favourite time of day was the crisp misty morning air, puffing steam as we talked, and listening to the town waking up ... roosters crowing, baby lambs bleating, birds chirping and bread vans doing their rounds.

Watching the sunrise is magic, and walking amid the hauntingly beautiful mist covered fields transports you to another place in your mind. Your lungs expand with the scent of Spain, life is slow, and your feet play a rhythmic tune on the gravel. It's like being in a movie set with the sun coming up showing the silhouette of the trees. The frogs and birds provide the soundtrack and you end up with sensory overload with the smells, the sights and the sounds. It is intoxicating.

The connection with the earth, the power and imprint of thousands of pilgrims who have walked the path before you, is overwhelming at times.

Learning to adapt to the pilgrim life becomes easier and it doesn't take long to master the basic Spanish needed to order a meal or find a bed.

The Spanish people are so kind and helpful, and they are brought up to respect the pilgrims walking to Santiago. Spain is a very religious country. It humbles you greatly. You learn to listen more, share more, observe more and learn how easy it is to live with so little.

It is just simplicity.

Yes, the Camino changes you. It nurtures you and calms your mind.

There is an ancient teaching about the ever flowing river of life carrying us forward and how we can never put your foot in the river in the same place twice. The water of the past has already flowed on. We need to go with the flow and embrace what is offered. The Camino helps you to do this.

It re-charges your batteries and re-sets your thoughts. It reminds you of what is important in life and leaves you with better intentions and stirs your desires for a more fulfilling life. It leaves us with the desire to be a better person, be more aware of our surroundings and to take time to appreciate life.

Everyone walks for their own reasons, whether it be spiritual, physical or emotional, but like the scallop shell with its lines all coming together in one spot, people gather in the Cathedral square in Santiago, the destination we all have in common … the supposed resting place of St James.

And then there is Finisterre, a small fishing village on the coast, and for many, the real end of the Camino. Here, feeling the power of the ocean, the gale force wind and the energy of the earth, you cannot help but be affected.

The Camino follows the earth's ley lines and its roof is the *Milky Way*. It mysteriously calls you and pulls you westward, sweeping you up in its energy. You are treated to the sounds of cuckoos, cowbells, frogs, and birds, scents of wild rosemary, fennel, eucalyptus and the sweet smell of cow dung.

Everyone wants to know why you walk the Camino when it pushes you to your limits and devours you in its beauty at the same time. The answer is simple … you must answer when it calls you. It is obviously a time for reflection on your self-worth and your life.

Just go!

About Margaret Caffyn

Margaret Caffyn (nee Stott) was born in Melbourne, Australia.

Her childhood was an adventure in itself, living in suburbia during the week and spending every weekend and school holidays at the family's sheep farm on Phillip Island. Maggie was christened, confirmed and educated in the Church of England.

Most people have a huge party when they turn 60 but Maggie took off and walked the Camino de Santiago, an 890 km trek from France to Santiago de Compostela in north western Spain.

Since then, she has walked the 1,300 km *Via de la Plata*, the *Portugues, Ingles* and part of the *Le Puy* route in France. Although now of no religion to speak of, she has experienced something quite unexplainable and ethereal on the Camino. It changed her life dramatically and has lead to some surprising opportunities.

In her lifetime, she has had many transformations. She has been a stenographer, medical secretary, waitress, cook, and function organiser. She owned a catering business and also a Mexican restaurant, and also works as a Remedial Massage therapist when at home. Margaret has recently been working up in the Blue Mountains at Glenella Guesthouse as a *host*, and also helped to organise the *2018 AusCamino Festival*. She has two children and two grandchildren and lives on the stunning Mornington Peninsula in Victoria.

Marg's book, *Walking Back Home: Finding Clarity on the Camino* (2017) is available from:

Https://www.margaretcaffyn@hotmail.com
https://www.margaretcaffyn.com.au
margcaffyn@hotmail.com
Amazon *http://amzn.eu/jcmm6y2*

The Importance of Purpose

Maeve Samuels and Nathan Fox

Every year, the Camino de Santiago entices all kinds of people, from all over the globe, to walk its paths. It is this sheer gathering of people, that lays the foundation for the way of St James. The particular track that caught our eye, was the *Camino del Norte*, following all the way along the rugged northern coast of Spain, before cutting inland to Santiago.

It was the thought of being by the ocean and crossing through the delightful fishing towns of Spain that lured us to do this route, above any other.

After disembarking the small train into the border town of Irun, our eyes were not yet accustomed to seeking out the small symbolic yellow arrows. We spent the next hour scouring the dusty streets, but when eventually we spotted a flash of yellow on a brick wall, our journey had officially begun. This excitement and anticipation followed us all the way to Finisterre, minus a few bumps along the way.

With gallons of energy and grins from ear to ear, we set off at a pace. However, a mere one kilometre later, we had whipped out our first-aid kit to deal with the blisters. It was at this point we realised that our warm-up route from Tenterden to Rye, in south-east UK, had done little to break in two pairs of boots from the *Mountain* warehouse clearance-sale.

Nevertheless, we powered on with the help of *Compeed* and ascended into one of the steepest climbs of the journey.

The rest of the afternoon was spent amidst tree lined paths and vistas that shot out across the Basque country.

With youth on our side, we arrived in Pasajes de San Juan with an hour before the converted church was due to open. We took the winding stairs down to the water's edge and drank ice cold beers, proud of the efforts of our first days walking. Upon return to the hilltop albergue, we were pleasantly surprised to find that the beds were all now occupied and full of faces we had shot by earlier that day.

Lesson learnt – be sure to grab a bed before a beer!

Flash forward to 10pm, and our situation had not yet changed. What had changed, however, was our geography, as we found ourselves a further 10 kms down the road, in the lively town of San Sebastian! As luck would have it, we found a room just off the Camino principal, fell heavy into separate beds (a concept that would become very familiar in the coming days) and in moments were out to the world. With a little wine in our bellies and tapas still digesting, our muscles and bones began to recover for the following days adventure.

The albergues were our daily refuge and sanctuary, they provided us with much needed rest and a chance to get to know other travellers - it was there at the close of each day that we shared some of our most precious moments surrounding some of life's most simple pleasures: food, wine and laughter.

One of the albergues that came when we needed it most, was in Orion. With a lush green garden overlooking the valley, everyone relaxed and soaked up the last of evening rays, while writing their journals or doing yoga.

Our favourite past time of an evening, was to massage each other's sore feet! Charming.

Leaving Orion behind us, we made for Deba with our new Spanish friend Chari, a lovely woman who became a great friend and let us stay a night with her in her apartment in Bilbao. The following days glided by effortlessly as we soaked in the unmistakable greenery and history of the Basque country.

After a lengthy few days on the track we blew into Comillas after a good mornings walk. The town was alive with various street performers and the general hustle and bustle of Spanish towns on a Saturday morning.

A young man juggling caught our eye and after a few minutes watching, we ended up back on the way with him and his friends. We took the beach path right down to the coast, out along the crashing waves. An afternoon spent with our toes in the cool ocean water and sand, ended with us leaving our new friends lunching on the beach, as the skies threatened to cave in. Our carefree companions did not seemed fazed and waved us good-bye to return to their lunches of jamon and bread.

As we neared San Vicente de la Baquera, the skies came through on their promise and the heavens opened. The warmth of September had meant shorts and t-shirts were our usual attire, however, this change had given us a good excuse to put on our brand new anoraks, and we plodded on quite happily in the rain.

As it turns out, we may as well have still been in shorts and t-shirts, as when we arrived in St Vincente we were thoroughly drenched! The thought of trying to dry our clothes off in a hostel that evening had no appeal, so we decided to splash a bit more cash for the luxury of a hot shower and a private room.

Luckily, we came across Hotel Luzon, a charmingly traditional two star, right in the centre of town. We didn't leave those walls for two days, aside from nipping out for some food here and there – it seemed this luxury was just slightly too hard to let go of.

It's safe to say that walking the track puts you in your own little bubble - eating when hungry, swimming in the sea and walking amidst beautiful landscapes. Walking into Bilbao really was a return to reality, casting us back into the life we'd come here to escape. For that reason, we would make visits to cities brief and would avoid heavy areas of industry at all costs, often taking buses and trains to do so (much to some other walkers chagrin). Some nights we would hear stories around the table of these infamous pilgrims who would take public transport. In these instances we would nod along, laughing inside, but in our hearts we didn't feel bad, as we were there for the experience and, to us, that didn't mean walking every inch.

Under the sweltering heat on the road to Gernika, we happened upon a young German man named Simon. The encounter that day would lead to us to bumping into Simon at every opportunity. Not always taking the same routes or staying in the same hostels, the chances of meeting were not always high, yet when it came to us and Simon it quickly seemed that no matter where he was, we'd be too.

Boat crossings, markets, off- roads and even at the crack of dawn in the middle of nowhere, Simon would be there. Though a simple memory, the people we met were as memorable for us as the road itself. So, if you are reading this Simon, please forgive us for not returning your lunch box.

Joined by Maeve's Mum and Auntie in Ribadeo we spent the last ten days walking into Galicia with a refreshing change of pace and a focus, now more than ever, on the regional cuisines and rioja. After 20 days on the road, we realised that we had become somewhat expert *Caminoers*.

We found delight in sharing with them everything we had learnt on our travels, like saying *Buen Camino!* to your fellow pilgrims, and how to book beds in Spanish over the phone. Louise, an avid bird-watcher, revelled in the air-borne wildlife of the region and we loved finally having someone to share their knowledge! Barbara, Maeve's mum, was right at home from day-one and took every chance to soak in the culture, dive into some good books, meet the locals and even try to perfect her Spanish pronunciation (though we never quite figured out how to say Guitiriz).

At dawn of our final days walk, we set off and joined other tired legs and dusty eyes back out on the Camino. The track was dark but headlamps and murmurs led the way. We traced through the tree-lined track to begin with, trying not to trip over the roots beneath our feet. It felt so special to be setting off at that hour, and the same feelings of excitement that we had felt on day one, had returned.

We stopped at a café with about 5 kms to go, and Barbara treated us all to a delicious breakfast so that we all had lots of energy for the final stretch.

As we neared closer, growing numbers of coloured back-packs could be seen for miles ahead, as all of the different routes merged in to one.

Some with flags and shells and others more simple. Sweaty backs lined heavy packs and recycled socks clung to well-used calves. Conversation in all different languages and laughter filled the air. Long highways turned into busy streets and the cobbled paths led us nearer. Like bees to a hive, pilgrims hovered and swarmed in the streets, taking photos, hugging one another and breathing a sigh of relief.

The ache in our bodies subsided momentarily as joy and exhilaration consumed us. The sheer size of the Cathedral was immense, however, we can't say much for its outer beauty as, much to our amusement, it was all under repair!

From the windy days where we traced the coast to the sunny afternoons where we ditched our packs and dipped our feet in the sea.

Taking the time to experience this part of the world left its mark on us, and is, in our opinion, one of the greatest gifts someone can give themselves, at any age or any time.

To spend each day with the simple purpose of getting from one place to the next and sharing in the pleasure of just being together, left us feeling more content than ever before.

This simplicity reflects, perhaps, what we should all strive for in life and highlights the importance of living with a purpose.

So, here's to the doors that welcomed us in and to the locals of Spain that always showed us the way.

About Maeve Samuels and Nathan Fox

Maeve Samuels, a 19 year old English girl who, born in London, moved to a small town called Tenterden in Kent, south-east UK when she was five years old.

Being the youngest of three, by 18 she was eager to follow their lead and get out into the world to explore. Consequently, she has filled the following few years with doing and learning as much as possible. The likes of walking the *Camino del Norte*, doing a ski season in St Anton, and taking on New Zealand in a van for three months are only a fraction of the fun included.

A product of her parents, it is in her nature to explore, adventure and surround herself with positive, like-minded people. In a few years' time, she wishes to return to the UK to put all of her energy into study physiotherapy, a career that has fascinated her from a young age.

Nathan Fox, a physiotherapy student from Wellington, currently living in Auckland, has spent the last four years in Europe, in which he spent the best part of it eating great cheeses, learning French and attempting to walk extremely long distances, whilst working and living in some of Europe's best kept secrets.

For Nathan, returning to his home country has been a long time coming so it is of no surprise that he's loving the chance to see family and friends again and explore New Zealand one pie at a time!

Spirit Calling

Monika Mundell

On the 9th of August, 2015… John and I were greeted by a misty, rainy morning as we woke up eager and excited to begin our first Camino from the doorsteps of our hostel in Saint Jean Pied de Port, France.

We felt like little children on Christmas morning.

The atmosphere was festive and sacred. I still remember how we stood there, our packs loaded to capacity, grinning at each other with tears of gratitude streaming down our faces.

Our Camino was about to get real. After years of dreaming, voraciously consuming Camino books and asking dozens of questions in forums, we were off.

Finally! Woohoo!

It all started with a casual comment from a friend. And it sparked a four-year dream of walking the Camino. Why was I so keen to walk the Camino and become a pilgrim? For me it's always been for the purpose of spiritual growth and to give myself a personal health challenge.

Before embarking on this amazing adventure I didn't know whether I could finish the Camino or how far I'd manage to walk.

In 2006, I was diagnosed with a potential life-threatening rare immune disorder in which my body's immune system attacked my nerves. Yeah! It was scary because I lost pretty much all the feeling in my legs and feet for three months.

And even so I eventually bounced back to good health, I was still experiencing recurring symptoms from time to time years later.

So despite my excitement I was cautious and somewhat scared that I may not make it to Santiago de Compostela. But I was yearning to become a pilgrim … to walk in silence for hours each day, and to listen to my body's wisdom, letting it be the compass that guided us along the path.

John, my amazing husband and fellow pilgrim was bursting with health and energy and I had no doubt that he would make it. We both knew that my body would set the pace. And we were fine with that.

The adventure had begun.

Our plan? To walk the *Camino Francés* across the Pyrenees into Spain and walk to Santiago de Compostela (then onwards to Cape Finisterre, a rock-bound peninsula on the west coast of Galicia, Spain).

We had allocated 60 days for the entire Camino, including rest days. We had read the books that told us that the average pilgrim needs about 35 days to walk the entire 800km long Camino de Santiago, aka the Way of St James.

Contrary to popular choice we decided to go slow. We wanted to make time to explore the villages along the way and to enjoy our pilgrimage, without pressure. In hindsight, it was a great decision.

We knew through our research that the Camino is personal, for every pilgrim. Meaning, the Camino experience is yours to make. You make it yours, regardless of the route you walk or the time it takes. Many pilgrims do the Camino in stages. They may walk 100km one year and then come back to continue the next. We were ready to do it all in the one go.

John and I carried 12kg backpacks. Looking back, our packs were too heavy. The pack weight also included 1.5 litres of water per person. I had packed my laptop too because I was walking the Camino while looking after my coaching clients. And I couldn't do this with *just* a mobile phone.

John wanted to blog about our journey. So he too carried his laptop. The laptop made it easier for him to upload photos at the end of each day and to write in comfort.

So yes, we lugged two 13-inch *MacBook Air* laptops with us for the entire Camino. Plus chargers and international power plugs. And no, I don't advise you do the same, because you can easily save about 4kgs in weight. In fact, the next time I walk the Camino I will do so without a laptop, because that extra weight has a habit of slowing you down, and draining your energy when you want to speed up.

Experience has shown me that working at the end of a long hike is not just challenging (due to connectivity issues)... it's crazy, too. Because when you arrive at the hostel, after a long hike, you just want a shower, to wash your clothes, have a quick nap and then use the little energy you have left to explore the village, before eating your pilgrim dinner. And then, you fall into bed exhausted but happy at around 8pm. A pilgrim's life!

Through drizzly rain we walked out of Saint Jean Pied de Port towards the *Refuge Orisson*, our rest stop for the first night. I'm so glad we had booked our bed at the *refuge*, because there was no way in hell I would have managed to walk all the way to Roncesvalles (on the other side of the Pyrenees Mountains) in just one day.

Little did we know that our Camino would turn into a pilgrimage of pain which resulted in daily (new) blisters for my poor feet and having to dig deep into my psyche to find the spirit and strength to keep walking ... while being surrounded the entire time by Spain's magnificent natural beauty.

How I love that country and its people! Despite having also experienced the not-so-pleasant side of rural Spain. Read on to know why.

Along the path we met amazing pilgrims from around the world. Each person had their own personal reasons to walk the Camino. Some were struggling with their marriage. Others were seeking answers for life-changing questions.

Along the way we gathered our own little Camino family: a ragtag of ladies from different walks of life, with whom we walked almost the entire Camino. Some of us started walking on the same day, at the same hostel, and finished together, in Santiago de Compostela.

Being surrounded by these special people really made our Camino extra special. We felt loved, appreciated and connected the whole time.

But truthfully, my pilgrimage was incredibly challenging for me because of my blisters. No matter what I tried to get rid of them, the blisters kept coming. So I pretty much walked the entire Camino with blisters.

Yet, despite the pain and discomfort I would do it all again tomorrow.

Walking the Camino has grown my inner strength and resilience. It's helped me become a better person. It taught me about gratitude for the simple pleasures in life. It taught me patience for living fully present in each moment and helped me rediscover the joys of celebrating the simple things—like warm showers, comfortable beds that are free of bed bugs, pilgrim meals, sweat-free clean clothes and the laughter, friendship and happiness of new friends.

I'm no saint. Nor am I religious. I believe that we're spirits in human bodies, here to have a human experience that helps us evolve. Walking the Camino has helped me connect with my ancestors and open myself up to the possibilities. I'm not lying when I say that despite my body's discomfort and pain my soul experienced only delight and happiness the entire time.

These feelings of joy, bliss, gratitude, fulfilment and connection to all that is are hard to explain to someone who hasn't experienced their own Camino. But I can say that I'm yearning to go back and I know that it's just a matter of time before we will walk the Camino again.

Despite all of the highlights and insights I've personally experienced while walking the Camino there were also some lowlights. Like rescuing two baby kittens from certain drowning and trying to find a new home for them.

It was a traumatic experience. Because every door we knocked on we were met with hostility and comments like, "Kill them, they're a pest."

I know. Different country, different rules. But still. Who in their right mind can knowingly kill two innocent baby kittens? We couldn't, and so we persisted until the kittens found a loving new home.

We also happened to be in Astorga when they found the body of the poor American pilgrim who was murdered. The news crews were positioned smack bang in the middle of our path interviewing people as we walked past. It created a lot of anxiety for the women on the Camino, me included. Sadly, safety is paramount for every pilgrim and it's scary when the peace and tranquility gets shattered by something as traumatic as murder.

The event prompted many pilgrims to buddy up for the day. Which I think is a good thing, because we can all learn a lot from each other. And when you walk with a stranger and part as friends it sure is a special feeling and experience.

Looking back I still think about our Camino years later. The experienced has affected me in ways I never anticipated and left a lasting impression that continues to feed me spiritually. Walking the Camino is even more special than you see in the movies and read about in books such as this one. It's life-changing.

If you're reading this short story of how the Camino changed my life and affected me (and John) deeply, on levels we didn't know existed, know this: if you're inspired to follow in our footsteps, do it.

Pack light. Wear good shoes. Choose a great backpack. And open your mind. You will not regret it.

But most importantly, don't rush.

I personally don't think I would have enjoyed the 35-day pace to Santiago. Slowing down has enriched my experience and even though John is much fitter than I am, he also commented on how he loved that we took the extra time to explore and enjoy our Camino. Take your time to enjoy the way. You'll never know what you'll find!

Buen Camino.

About Monika (Nika) and John Mundell

Nika and John walked from Saint Jean Pied de Port to Santiago de Compostela, and then onto Cape Finisterre—roughly 890 km—in 55 days, which included five rest days. They averaged about 15 kms a day and each carried a 34 lt *Deuter Act Trail Pro* backpack, which they loved and would buy again.

Nika and John are two Australian entrepreneurs in search of freedom and a liberated lifestyle. In March 2014, they waved goodbye to their home, investment properties, fancy car, pets, good friends and a coastal lifestyle, to break up the monotony of suburbia and realise their life-long dream of being location independent.

Why?

Because they have an insatiable desire to feel ALIVE and break with conformity. Nika and John are passionate about travel and exploring new cultures. And they want to encourage and empower you to crush your boredom and live an invigorated life.

Visit Nika's website where she helps badass business women manifest more soul clients and explode their magik and profits:

https://www.polarizeandprofit.com/

Or subscribe to John's blog to stay posted on their adventures, where you can find daily entries for their Camino:

https://entrepreneursodyssey.com/

You can also friend them on Facebook where you can find them sharing their adventures and life:

@monikamundell and *@johnmundell*

Friends Along The Way

Dan Stains

One week in 2012, as part of our family tradition of hiring a DVD from the local *Video Ezy*, accompanied by munching on ice-cream and popcorn, we chose to watch *The Way*. The movie stars Martin Sheen as Dr. Thomas Avery, the father of Daniel, a free-spirited adventurer, played by Sheen's real-life son, Emilio Estevez.

In a freak accident, Daniel is killed in treacherous conditions while crossing the Pyrenees on his way to Santiago de Compostela. Tom, Martin Sheen's character, arrives in France to collect his sons remains, however once there, he decides to honour his son Daniel by walking the Camino on his behalf with the intention of sprinkling his son's ashes along the way.

The scenery and plot captivated my imagination and I wanted to do what Martin Sheen had done; explore the south of France, climb the Pyrenees and walk across the north of Spain to this amazing cathedral where pilgrims worshipped the Patron Saint of Spain, Saint James. My partner at the time was a trekker and aware of the Camino and suggested I read up on it to see if it was something we could do together. The legend of *The Camino* and my desire to walk it had been sown.

The first book I read was *To The Field Of Stars* by Catholic priest, Kevin A Codd, who had walked the Camino and gave his insights into what it meant to him. He explained the whole history of the Camino, how it became a pilgrimage and why it was important for Catholics to make this trek. Even the name of the pilgrim destination Camino De Santiago De Compostela was romantically spelled out. How could an old Catholic boy, resist falling in love with the concept of *'The way of Saint James of the field of stars'*?

Imagine the benefits: walking freely and anonymously in France and Spain, eating delicious three-course meals for lunch and dinner whilst drinking *vino tintos* daily. However, what clenched the deal was the promise of having my soul cleansed and my sins forgiven for the next year.

The constant theme from the different authors suggested you had to have a strong reason for walking the Camino. They all stated it must be stronger than simply wanting to walk the distance to brag to family and friends.

The common theme and running joke from most people walking the Camino was for one of the three D's: DIVORCE, DIET or DEPRESSION.

I wasn't sure which category I fell into but it did seem to be an appropriate fit for a lot of people along the path. For the life of me I tried and persisted to engineer and create a purpose, all to no avail, I just simply wanted to be like Martin Sheen and walk this magical path without help in any way.

We arrived in St Jean Pied De Port the day before we were due to set out on our *Camino Francés*. This allowed us to purchase our *Pilgrim Passport* and get a rough idea of what the next day's trek would include.

The passport is paramount and requires stamping along the route, allowing the trekker to stay in the albergues (Spanish term meaning hostel) which is one of the choices a pilgrim has for accommodation along the route.

The dormitory style room, consisting of multiple double bunk beds, the number of which was dependent on the size of the room, ranged in price from a donation (*donación*) of your choice and up to around €15 for a top of the range residence. The average price was €10 per night.

The cost of dining on a three-course meal in most of the villages was €10, couple this with a high-quality bottle of *vino tinto* selling for around €2-€3.

I quickly understood why the Camino rates in the Top 5 budget holiday destinations of the world. You can safely budget on spending around €40 per day to live like a king.

We were warned the first day's hike to Roncesvalles is treacherous, 29 kms in total, half going over Pyrenees, the same route Napoleon took to conquer Spain, I was told.

Not only did you have to battle the effects of altitude and the 14-15 kms of continuous vertical walking, your knees were then forced to cope with 14-15 kms of the constant pressure of downward hiking.

We were tough, after all in a previous life I had been a Professional Rugby League player, representing Australia and Queensland in *State of Origin*. Surely it would be a breeze as we had spent months preparing ourselves physically. Eight kilometres in and according to the guide book we had arrived at Orison, the first and only food stop before Roncesvalles. The guide book had it marked as a village, however the only thing at this place was an albergue. It was lunch time so we decided to venture in, have a short rest, some lunch and then make our way to Roncesvalles.

Well that was the plan.

Big mistake ... or was it?

We shared our table with people from all over the world. There was a beautiful couple (Kevin and Robin from Alaska) who, like Jen and I, were about to embark on their first Camino; an older man, Angle and his two sons from the Netherlands; Helmut a German scholar who I'm sure fell into one of those *D categories*; Jayne and Susie, two beautiful air hostesses from Canada; Lari and Hedley, wonderful experienced hikers from Perth Australia; as well as another great couple from Sydney, Australia, Nick and Helen.

I was most intrigued by a group of three very beautiful Irish ladies (Grainne, Ger and Sinead) along with their three teenage sons (Ian, Misael and Adam) playing this drinking game called *spoons*. It didn't take long for the whole room to join in, it was so much fun.

We all sat around the lunch table, playing the game, drinking *vino tintos* and listening to everyone's personal stories. I loved being in their company and I'm so glad we stayed in Orison that first night as this really set the scene for our wonderful Camino experience.

The next day's hike was very tough for a couple of reasons. Obviously the *vino tinto* consumed the day before made the day a little blurry. Along with this we still had another 8 kms of mountains to climb before the 13 kms of downward hiking.

We finally arrived the next afternoon, Easter Sunday in Roncesvalles and experienced what for me was the most amazing Easter Sunday Mass service. The little stone church was packed to the rafters with pilgrims from all over the world celebrating Easter Sunday together.

The Irish ladies and their boys stayed with us for another ten wonderful days, where we shared beautiful communal meals and relived some of the funny events of each day. Grainne's father had walked the Camino and she had good knowledge of the best places to stop and which albergue would give us the most entertaining experience. Grainne's son, Ian, spoke fluent Spanish, allowing him to ring ahead, assuring us each a bed at some of the more popular albergues.

Aside from raising my boys and witnessing them grow into happy, healthy, young men; following the little yellow arrows to the Cathedral of Santiago de Compostela rates as one of my top all-time achievements.

Was it a walk in the park? No, not at all. It was tough and I quickly began to comprehend why previous pilgrims stated with conviction the need for a strong purpose to undertake the Camino.

It took between 7-10 days for my body to become accustomed to the weight of my backpack and the constant walking. Tendonitis and blisters were common meal time discussions. In fact, each morning I would wake to the noise of the rustling sound of blister packs containing *Ibuprofen* being popped opened. This was by far the most popular purchase of medication whilst on the Camino.

It became a game to see who could find the most powerful tablet on the trek. 600mgs, three times the strength of anything we found over the counter in Australia, became the record find.

Jen digested two of these beauties and a coffee with breakfast. That day's walk quickly became a canter. The 17,000 words that the typical woman is supposed to use daily were completed in the first hour. These tablets suddenly became very popular amongst the pilgrims once the word spread.

In Shirley MacLaine's book, *The Camino: A Journey of the Spirit* (2000) she talks about every person having what she termed *energy meridians*. According to Eastern philosophy, they are a sophisticated network of energy pathways, or super highways where every living creature's vital life force (chi) flows. Every living being, Shirley believed, reflected *Mother Earth*, meaning our earth had these energy meridians - *ley lines* - as well.

It just so happened the Camino path followed one of the earth's energy meridians which may explain why it is regarded as a healing pilgrimage. I don't know a lot about Eastern philosophy, however, at times there did seem to be elevated levels of spiritual energy.

At the beginning, pilgrims were excited, looking for ways to contribute to others. As the Camino levelled out along the Meseta (Spanish for plateau, a highland plateau, middle part of The Camino) pilgrim's energy also plateaued, then once hitting Portomarin, 100 kms from Santiago I noticed a dramatic rise in energy.

Three hours into a day's walk we came to an ancient stone church where a beaming priest was standing, adorned in his robes. He couldn't contain his joy for life, smiling as if he was witnessing the second coming.

There was no option but go in and greet this beautiful soul. It would have been an un-Christian act to exit without a donation and a photo. Robin arranged for the priest to be centre stage surrounded by all of us.

With me on one side and Jen on the other, holding us for what seemed an eternity.

He kept asking for more photos and squeezing me tighter and tighter.

As we commenced back on the trail, I was still moved by the priest holding us and praying for our sins, when a fellow pilgrim joked about the length of time the photo took. I was still smiling in the glow of the experience, blissfully unaware until Jen quietly mentioned, that the priest was rubbing her butt the whole time. Amusingly, reiterating that each experience can truly differ from one pilgrim to the next.

The last morning of our walk into Santiago was a mix of exhilaration and sadness. I was excited to reach our destination, however, I also realized it signalled the end of our journey. One we had shared with so many wonderful new friends.

The most common question asked by budding pilgrims is: *"What advice would you give to someone preparing to walk the Camino?"*

Very simply, it is the same advice I give my sons: look after your body and particularly your feet. The Camino does not discriminate.

Being a professional athlete in a previous life, doesn't make you better equipped to handle what the Camino will throw at you. The body cannot carry the extra weight of an individual's ego. You *must* unpack it before you leave home. Each day is precious and each day is different. You don't know what your body or mind will require tomorrow. What worked last week or yesterday won't necessarily work today. Today is different and your needs are different. Listen to what is required of you today.

The second question asked of me is: *"Would I do anything different?"*

Possibly, or maybe not. After all, if things were different I may not be where I am now, telling you my story. So no, I wouldn't change a thing. I loved every minute of my Camino and cherish the memories and friends I met along *The Way*.

About Dan Stains

Dan Stains is a commercial real estate professional, successfully negotiating nearly $6,000,000 of sales in the first 12 months of his real estate career.

Dan's sporting career commenced as a professional Rugby League player with the *Cronulla Sharks* and then the *Balmain Tigers* in Sydney, representing both QLD in the *State of Origin* and Australia against New Zealand.

He then turned his hand to coaching where he led the *Tigers* reserve grade team to the grand final in his first year. He then was recruited by Richard Branson's *London Broncos* taking them to their maiden *Challenge Cup Final* at London's famous Wembley Stadium.

Returning to Australia in 2000, Dan chose the Sunshine Coast to live and raise his family, where he owned and managed a business for 13 years before turning his hand to developing land in Maroochydore.

During this time, Dan has established relationships with business owners and understands the needs and frustrations of both the owners and buyers in the real estate market leading him to pursue a career as a real estate professional.

With Dan's passion and long history of buying and selling both residential and commercial real estate in Sydney, Toowoomba and the Sunshine Coast, Australia, it is no surprise his knowledge is unsurpassed in this field.

Dan can be contacted by email *danstains@atrealty.com.au* or by phone on *+61 (0) 455 664-445*.

About Dan Stains

Dan Stains is a commercial real-estate professional, successfully negotiating nearly $6,000,000 of sales in the first 12 months of his real estate career.

Dan's sporting career commenced as a professional Rugby League player with the Canberra Raiders and then the Broncos. Dan in 1990s represented Australia in the World and Australia against New Zealand.

How An Ancient Path Led Me To My True Self

Heather Waring

I began my Camino journey, in October 2008, inspired by the book *Clear Waters Rising* by Nicholas Crane. I sat with the idea of walking the *Camino Francés*, not sure how to make it happen, until a chance discussion with a fellow walker made it clear that this was something we both wanted to do.

Lifestyles didn't allow us to take 4-6 weeks away so we decided to increase the length of the journey and start our adventure in the centre of France in the town of Le Puy en Velay, one of the three starting points for the Camino de Santiago in France.

Walking approximately a week a year, we would return to the place we had finished in and pick up the path from there. Someone once said to me how much they respected my determination at doing it this way and how much harder it must be.

I had never seen it that way but on reflection, I believe it has actually allowed me to savour the miles/kms and experiences of each section more fully. The decision to do it in this way is one I am eternally grateful for, as it has allowed me to get to know both the French and Spanish sections of this great long distance path and to be able to advise on both pulling out the contrasts and similarities. I now get great joy from being able to introduce many women to both sections through my *Camino Experiences*.

I am not a religious person so wanting to walk the Camino was driven by something else. For me, as a passionate long distance walker, it was the challenge; the opportunity to walk a famous route and the experience of all it has to offer in terms of the history, the scenery, the buildings and the food and wine.

On the path and on this journey there are two things that made a huge impact on me and continue to do so. They are now integrated into my everyday life and are a key part of how I live my life and run my business.

The first one is *Solitude*.

Many choose to make this journey alone, although in reality one is very rarely physically alone, especially on the Spanish side where the popularity of the route now attracts thousands of pilgrims a year. According to the Confraternity of St James 301,036 pilgrims collected their Compostela (Pilgrim Certificate) in 2017.

However, even though I chose to walk with a female friend, we both enjoyed periods of solitude. We would walk side by side but often engaged in our own thoughts and we would also choose to walk physically alone, sometimes needing that space to enable our thinking and mental exploration.

I am someone who loves the mystery of a path when there are hills or mountains, when the path twists and turns through woodland or veers off round a corner, I am intrigued by what I am going to find on the other side. By comparison, my least favourite path is a long straight one that I can see stretching out into the distance affording no mystery at all and scarily no place where I might disappear into to pee!! On the Camino you will find both.

On paths such as this I have different ways of dealing with them and that will often depend on my frame of mind. Sometimes I turn to mantras to get me through. One of my favourites is *'I walk with ease and flow, pain free with every step'.*

On some sections in times of my burnout, the subsequent adrenal fatigue had manifested itself in joint pain and while movement was what was needed, it wasn't always easy. Chanting to myself in this way got me through many miles and for me, made that part of the journey easier.

However, by doing this am I looking for the easy way out? Some would say that you need to open yourself up to this discomfort rather than to run from it. Those deeply religious and those on the Camino to find themselves may indeed welcome these times as a chance to delve deep. Perhaps this is one of the gifts the Camino brings. Indeed, I have also taken this route at times and found previously untapped ideas surfacing but also deeply buried feelings have been uncovered. I have not always been brave enough to go within and you know that's ok, because I believe that the timing too has to be right. If you have experienced this, go easy on yourself, the right time will come.

And another thing to add, when leaving this solitude behind I have been grateful for the ear of my walking buddy as well as the hugs and support. Allow that to happen and you will find that the need to look at the path ahead and not to maintain eye to eye contact, makes it much easier to share your burdens with others and often someone you hardly know.

The second issue I want to raise is *Spirituality*.

I would describe myself as spiritual and as I have walked the Camino I have become more so. There are many definitions of spirituality, for me it is about connection, connection with something greater than me but also connection with myself and this life that I am living. Being in nature plays a great role here. You could say in some ways that Nature has become my god. Indeed it is to the Universe and to Mother Nature that I give thanks every morning as I stand on my yoga mat. And no matter now many times I walk sections of this inspiring path, I can always find something new to marvel at and to photograph.

I love to embrace all that each day on the path offers. Usually it includes the opportunity to meet someone new or to talk further with someone I met previously. Daily, it's the chance to visit the many churches on the journey, those that are large cathedrals as in Burgos, Leon and Santiago; the abbeys of France and the many small churches, sometimes only made up of one room. They offer shelter from the weather, calm and peace and stories of history and refurbishment.

But mostly, for me, it's the beauty of nature that unfolds.

The springtime of flowers, growth and newness; the transhumance where the animals are moved from one grazing ground to another so up to the higher pastures for the summer and returned to the lower land in winter and in the autumn, the pleasure of walking through the vineyards where the grapes hang heavily on the vines and where the grape picking may have already started.

Walking in nature and practicing mindful walking and walking mediation as I do myself and with my clients, has made me more grounded and ensures that I spend more of my time being in the moment.

In today's fast paced life, full of expectations and overwhelm being able to connect to the power and majesty of nature is such a calming action. How often do we, especially women, get the time to put ourselves first and to walk and reflect on our lives? This is the one factor that all of the women I walk this path with, comment on. The path and nature helps to put things into perspective. Having slogged up to the top of a hill in heat, wind or rain, perhaps having wondered if you'd ever make it, there is time to stop, slow down the heart rate and look out onto a piece of this great world. When this happens to me, I am reminded of how small and insignificant I really am and how often the things I get caught up in, and with, are not worth worrying about. It's sobering and helpful.

On all of the Camino I am reminded of the many who have walked before, many who walked as a penance, many who were desperately ill and many who were attacked and robbed along the way.

Nowhere did this strike me more than on the last section from Sarria to Santiago.

I was pleasantly surprised at the greenery but this of course is Galicia, *green Spain* and as I walked through miles and miles of ancient oak woods I found myself wondering about the stories that these gnarled trees could tell if only they could talk. I found myself wanting to spend more time walking ancient paths. I believe that there is a great wisdom in these paths, wisdom and stories that can enhance our own lives and that lead us to tap into our own wisdom, and uncover our own stories. We may not always realise or value what we bring, we may need help to gently unravel what is buried and assistance to shape and develop it but our stories are there and should be shared.

Walking makes my heart and my soul sing and my years walking the Camino in times when I have been really fit and in times when I have been less so, have been my sanity. I know that my annual escapes to this path played a role in my burnout recovery and my regular returning to it reminds me of the need to look after me. It also reminds me of all I have learnt and how far I have come.

Once, I was the woman who tried to detox in January and February and wondered why it was so hard. Who hated February because it was cold and grey and nondescript and who pushed herself all year round. I am now the woman who lives her life in line with the cycles of nature, who can spot fungi from great distances and who enjoys hibernation time from December to March when I go within. I write and I plan; I declutter; I read; I nourish my body and cosy up by the fire. This allows me to replenish and recharge for the other three seasons when I am sharing my Camino learning with others as I lead them on the path and when I explore the many other Camino paths such as the *Camino del Norte* and the *Camino Portugues* for my own personal interest and walk challenges.

There is a wonderful simplicity to life when you get up in the morning knowing that you have to get from where you are now, point A, to your destination, point B and probably the biggest decision that you are going to have to make is what to have for lunch or where to stop and eat it. All you have to do is give yourself to the day, open your eyes widely, take a deep breath in and let tension and anxiety go as you breathe out and put one step in front of the other.

Buen Camino, or as they say in France, *Bon Chemin*.

About Heather Waring

In 2013/ 2014 Heather suffered burnout and was diagnosed with Adrenal Fatigue which she describes as *the best and biggest gift* she could ever have been given.

Taking the opportunity to stop, Heather took time out to pause and reflect on her life and fully invest in her recovery.

As a result of that journey and with her passion for walking and coaching, she now gives women space to reflect by taking them on transformational walking experiences along ancient paths, like the Camino de Santiago where she facilitates their rediscovery and reconnection with the women they want to be and the life they wish to live.

Heather is a walk leader and certified coach and an active member of the *Athena Network*.

She has been a columnist for both *Cosmopolitan* magazine and the *Sunday Express*, a regular contributor to *Glamour* magazine and for two years she wrote a syndicated column for the *Newsquest* group. Heather has given radio and TV interviews and written many blog posts as well as being regularly interviewed for podcasts and blog and local radio.

To find out more visit:

http://womenwalkingwomentalking.com and especially
http://womenwalkingwomentalking.com/experiences/camino/
Facebook - https://www.facebook.com/womenwalking
womentalking/and https://www.facebook.com/heather.waring1
Twitter - https://twitter.com/heatherwaring
LinkedIn - https://uk.linkedin.com/in/heatherwaring
Pinterest - https://www.pinterest.com/heatherywaring/
Instagram - https://www.instagram.com/heatherywaring/

Against The Odds, Against The Current

Gabriella Ferenczi

End of September 2016, my other half and I embarked on a 300 km journey on foot, from León to Santiago de Compostela in Spain, through treacherous mountains and dry, stony plains, beautiful hills and deep forests, picturesque towns and abandoned villages – looking for … well, not sure what.

For us, it was all about leaving our busy London life behind for 16 days (the longest break we've ever taken away from our businesses so far) and seeing things from a different perspective, getting 'some' exercise to refresh our bodies and minds, and whatever happens to us – just let it be and take it all in.

León seemed to be the right starting point for the journey: 300 kms away from Santiago, 15 days in total from the actual start to the goal and then back to the airport.

That should be doable if we stick to a 15-20-25 kms average daily walk - we thought.

What we didn't know much about however were our physical capabilities. We don't really do sports in London, except I walk a lot in the City and Mr Ferenczi goes swimming occasionally. But that was it. Mentally, we were prepared for the journey. Physically – not so much.

We knew that packing for the Camino was not going to be easy, yet left everything literally to the last minute. We bought all the hiking stuff on the day before the journey. Adventurous and reckless? I guess we were a little bit of both in this instance, but honestly, we were so busy before the travel that we just couldn't find the time to go shopping anytime sooner.

Bearing the burden

We managed to get the packing right.

Shoes and backpack, the two most important things, were perfect, except for one thing: The backpack - once filled with the essentials, was incredibly heavy.

We also had to buy a few more stuff on the way which we only found out were missing when on the road: breathable shorts, knee protection, easily accessible holder for phone/camera, guide book, creams to ease muscle pain etc. You might say that these aren't that heavy – well, I can confirm that you do feel every single extra gram that's on your shoulders.

Third day on the way and about 50 kms behind us, the pain was excruciating.

In Astorga, we met fellow pilgrims who told us about their suffering of backache. They explained that they couldn't really enjoy the journey because of the heavy burden. Instead of admiring the view, they'd stare at the floor all the time while walking. We felt the same.

Some pilgrims reached a point where they decided to use a cheap transport service that took their heavy stuff to the next place where they'd planned to sleep, so they could walk freely and enjoy the Camino. We started to toy with the idea too.

But …

Both my husband and I are very protective of each other, our families, our belongings, our values, our everything.

We never really knew where we'd end up, how far we could go. It seemed impossible to tell in the morning where we'd spend the night. And even if, we wouldn't let go of our sh*t, would we? That backpack and each other was literally all we had!

We were tempted, really tempted to get our heavy stuff transported … but then, we figured this:

Our clothes and basic toiletries are all down to the absolute minimum, a sleeping bag is what gives us comfort for the night, so these really are the basic belongings of our life that, although heavy, are actually part of us. So let's embrace this and let's learn to enjoy the road, the view, the whole journey – despite the burden, with the burden.

And therefore, we decided to carry our sh*t ... all the way.

By Day 5, the pain was still there but it was different. On one hand, we got used to it and learnt to cope.

On the other hand, we accepted it as being an inseparable part of our journey and started to really enjoy and appreciate the Way.

To me, this has two symbolical meanings.

Life throws at us so many difficulties, and there are two possible ways to react: You either learn to cope and accept them, learn from them and get on with life. Or, you find the point when you say that it's enough, and find a solution to overcome those difficulties by eliminating certain things from your life you can cope without.

Both points are equally valid I believe, and the way you take is entirely down to you, no one can or should judge you.

We decided to do it the hard way, despite the lack of physical exercise beforehand, and we're really proud of our achievement. At the same time, we do understand and accept that there are indeed other ways to overcome challenging circumstances.

There's surely a point when you need to let go. Where you simply need to change, lessen the burden in order to be able to focus on other important things.

Where that point is, is something each and every one of us has to explore themselves.

The joy of being out of control

I am a big planner who likes to know what the day holds and schedules everything into the diary, but this time I challenged myself to take it real easy and let things happen to us, instead of us being behind the wheel as it usually is.

We set on the journey with no plan, no expectations, and no guide book.

All we knew was the date of our flight to get to Oviedo and the date of the flight back 16 days later. Other than that, nothing. We were not sure if we'd be able to reach our goal, Santiago, at all.

Because we hadn't had much physical exercise beforehand, we didn't really know how much time we'd need to walk 20-30 kms, let alone how much distance we'd actually be able to cover each day. Therefore, we didn't know where we'd end up sleeping each day.

Osea no ...

Most pilgrims leave their accommodation at dawn and reach their goal for the day by 2-3pm. We were the opposite: Leave at 10-11am, and arrive 6-7pm was our usual rhythm.

On Day 2, it was about 6pm when we had reached Santibáñez de Valdeiglesias, a tiny little village between León and Astorga, only to find no more accommodation left. At that time, we'd already had 20km behind us, but we had to continue, as there was no other option. We were told that it was going to be a long walk, and honestly, we were up for it.

The road was not very well marked in this section of the Camino. We got lost in the middle of nowhere, sunset fast approaching. Usually, you do see fellow pilgrims on the way. At this time of the day, there's no-one around.

Suddenly, we heard the voice of a car approaching - in the hills. We thought - wow. A car! Here?! Pablo* stopped, asked us where we were heading, said that we were crazy and offered us a lift to the nearest town Astorga - 10 kms away.

Dilemma, dilemma. Never sit in a stranger's car … yet, at that point, we were seriously starting to worry that there's not much time left until dark. Pablo only understood *yes* and *no* in English, so we had to try our best to navigate through the language barrier. We spoke very little Spanish, but quite soon understood that Pablo lived in a tent in the bushes.

To our surprise, he stopped after about 2 kms on the way so we could see *his place*. His hospitality included offering us interesting substances to try that would ease our pains and aches and guarantee a good mood. We kindly declined, he enjoyed a sniff or two. Then, we were supposed to continue the ride with him for the next 8 kms. *Osea, no* … (colloquial Spanish for: *I mean, no.*)

At that point, we kindly said goodbye and decided to continue our journey on foot. Pablo seemed to be a genuinely nice and helpful guy and that 2 kms lift saved us valuable time - and loads of painful steps, but there was no chance that we would continue with him. (From Pablo's place, we walked as fast as we could for the next couple of hours and reached Astorga at 9.15pm - it was completely dark.)

First thing before continuing our journey next day was to buy a good guide book.

Kindness: a language everyone understands

On Day 4, we reached Rabanal, a beautiful little village right before the iconic Cruz de Ferro. It turned out we didn't have enough cash on us to pay for our accommodation. Card payments were not accepted and in rural areas, cash machines are nowhere to be seen. Luckily, our kind host gave us a lift back to the nearest town.

I had to learn to accept that I can't solve everything on my own, that I need to ask for help, and yes, there are times when we are dependent on others.

This sense of trust, openness and channelling my own intuition was something that I had to rediscover. It was exhilarating and refreshing.

As I'm writing this, suddenly I remembered this beautiful thought from Paulo Coelho's book *The Pilgrimage* that I read a few weeks before our journey:

"When you travel, you experience, in a very practical way, the act of rebirth.

You confront completely new situations, the day passes more slowly, and on most journeys you don't even understand the language the people speak.

So you are like a child just out of the womb. You begin to attach much more importance to the things around you because your survival depends upon them.

You begin to be more accessible to others because they may be able to help you in difficult situations. And you accept any small favour from the gods with great delight, as if it were an episode you'd remember for the rest of your life.

At the same time, since all things are new, you see only the beauty in them, and you feel happy to be alive. That's why a religious pilgrimage has always been one of the most objective ways of achieving insight."

Coelho. P. (1997). *The Pilgrimage.* Thorsons

Letting things take their own natural course I learnt that sometimes, it's best to let go of plans, allow life to happen spontaneously and pay attention to what's happening.

"Only one who wonders finds new paths." Norwegian proverb

We reached Santiago on Day 15, in excruciating pain. After a little rest, we went to give a hug to St James in the cathedral, then rewarded ourselves with a lovely dinner in a traditional Galician restaurant, listened to some live piano music in the nearby hotel, and had a very restful sleep.

We attended the traditional Pilgrim Mass at 12 noon the next day and had to leave this beautiful town right afterwards in order to catch our evening flight from Oviedo back to the UK.

Practical Top Tips

- Buy a good guide book.
- Invest in great quality backpack and shoes. Don't spare money on that.
- Allow yourself time to spend in Santiago, at least a full day after your arrival.

*Pablo's name has been changed to protect and respect his privacy.

About Gabriella Ferenczi

Gabriella Ferenczi is a German and Hungarian language coach, founder of *ProLingua Global*, a London-based language training company.

Gabriella and her husband Viktor took 15 days to walk a 300 km section of the Camino, from León to Santiago de Compostela.

They reached Santiago on Day 15. The experience affected both of them deeply.

Gabriella is a linguist and language enthusiast. Her mission with *ProLingua Global* is to help UK businesses to operate more effectively in a global, multicultural and multilingual world, take advantage of more opportunities and strengthen international trade relationships.

Gabriella believes that learning a new language promotes understanding between people, businesses, countries and cultures. It bridges gaps and enables to build meaningful connections.

www.gabriellaferenczi.com
www.prolingua.global
info@gabriellaferenczi.com
LinkedIn: https://www.linkedin.com/in/gabriellaferenczi/
Facebook: https://www.facebook.com/
GabriellaFerencziOfficial/
Twitter: @GabiFerenczi
Instagram: @Gabriella.Ferenczi

A Journey of Self-Belief

Amanda Candy

Don't follow just to follow

On the first day heading up to Roncesvalles from St Jean Pied de Port I met a couple who were deciding to go one way where a sign said to head off the road. The woman wasn't sure the sign was real. I said I was going to go and head that way and see where it leads me. As I headed along the path I turned around to them and said, "Don't follow just to follow." They chose to continue along the road. Further into the Camino I ran into them again, they mentioned to me that what I had said to them had become their mantra for their walk and their life, choosing their own path and not following others.

I nearly didn't walk the Camino it was really only a vague idea that I had, something to consider until a better idea came along. Then I found myself in a shop looking at backpacks. There was a sort of hollowness about what I was doing as though my body wasn't really participating or my mind and soul. It all felt a bit blurry.

Then something shifted.

A guy came into the shop and he was going for a bit of a walk. Guess where to? Yup, the Camino.

I felt a tinge of envy, lucky guy I thought. Hang on, why the envy you're about to go and do the same walk. The spark began to ignite and OMG I can go walk the Camino as well, everything is set into place there is absolutely nothing stopping me from going other than myself. I walked out of the shop with the backpack on.

That's when the magic happened, something I had buried for a very long time began to awaken and slowly, very slowly I began to feel as though I was walking the Camino.

The memory of past walks came to mind and the feeling of freedom, challenge and joy moved into my veins. A small twinge of *I can do this* ran through my body. A light began to shine. An eagerness and excitement emerged.

Don't rush things

After several days of walking, I came upon a woman who was walking alone. She told me how she had begun her walk with her daughter and granddaughter but they had had to pull out. It turns out that the granddaughter who was around 18 was very fit and found the slow pace of walking challenging so she chose to run most of the way but after several days of running she experienced shin splints, excruciating blisters and had twisted her ankle badly making finishing impossible.

The mother then had to pull out to care for her daughter. The grandmother was left to finish on her own and was slowly methodically putting one foot in front of the other.

There is no one size fits all that works for this walk. We are all unique and what works for one may not work for you. It's not difficult to do and it can be as complicated or as simple as you want to make it.

What is required is a preparedness to look inside, to be honest with yourself to give yourself a fair go and when you do come out the other end you will truly be able to say, "*I've got this.*" My ego had such a strong hold on me before I started the walk that I was planning how many kilometres I could finish each day and in what time.

I wasn't focusing on the experience until a friend of mine pointed out my foolishness to me.

Walk your own walk

Sam met a lady on the first day and she and her friends walked a lot faster than he was used to. Not wanting to miss out on the connection he worked hard to keep up day after day.

He ended up with severe blisters and after a while had to stop for several days to allow them to heal. Because he was besotted with this woman he chose to catch a bus to catch up, therefore missing out on his goal of walking the entire way.

I'm a champion at helping other people believe in themselves. I was a complete fraud when I looked to find my own. Deep down I didn't believe I could finish the walk and I really needed to complete something that I started. I began creating all the excuses I could to sabotage myself. Hey, bung knee, no training, I get lost going outside my own front door. Who am I to think I can do this?

Then I thought *What if? What if I put one foot in front of the other continuously and see where it leads?*

The journey went from finishing something to a journey of self-belief. There are as many reasons for doing the Camino as there are people who walk it. After a few days, I stopped asking people why they were walking I thought it prudent to let them keep it to themselves.

It's OK to take a wrong turn

Early on I chose to ignore a sign as I liked the look of the other direction, so I walked for a few kilometres and the view was nice. But then I ended up exactly where I had started!

Feeling rather foolish a young man came along the path. We walked together briefly he told me how he had quit his job to do the walk. He had been feeling very bad about himself but one day he had the incredible opportunity to play music for the Pope. This in itself was an unbelievable opportunity coming from a small village. What inspired him to shift was seeing himself on TV playing in front of the Pope.

He saw a happy man and he wanted to be more like that.

The man was him and he knew he was hidden inside but he had seen a glimpse of who he could be.

This experience touched me so much. If I hadn't taken a wrong turn and walked that extra distance I would not have connected with this man and I would not have heard his story.

Align your goals

A group of women had chosen to do the walk together. They had all been friends for years. They felt it was important to walk everyday together. What they hadn't considered was each other's reason for doing the walk or their own unique pace.

One of them liked to rule the others and choose the direction they would take and the distances they would cover each day. One was easy going, so was happy to be guided. One didn't like it but kept it to herself letting things fester. And one decided early on to do her own thing which annoyed the others. This group didn't openly communicate their needs and sadly by the end, their friendship suffered.

I believe we are more capable then we give ourselves credit for.

I didn't believe I could finish the walk and yet I did, every step of it. There were difficult days and times when the joy I experienced was so incredible.

One day comes to mind. I call it *Windmill Day*. There were windmills in the fields though I don't remember where it was. The fields were filled with wheat and the wind was strong that day. And as I looked across the vista the wheat was dancing to the rhythm of the wind. The different colours and textures glistened from the sun: it was mesmerising.

God made the wind dance that day and it remains with me still.

Create your own community

One of the absolute joys of the Camino is the mix of people relating to each other from different walks of life, religions, ethnicity, values, viewpoints, opinions all with a common interest: *the walk*. The Camino breeds tolerance it helps people to connect that may not otherwise and it opens doors to new ideas. You can choose along the way to either mix with others or keep to yourself.

I chose to meet new people, to share my life with them and to listen to their stories. This is something that I do on a daily basis I've done that for years and I realised my life is actually like the Camino most of the time. Community is important to me.

One of the people I met along my journey said to me that I created a community wherever I go. This really stuck with me. The challenge for most people is to bring that connection into our day-to-day lives and to support others to do the same. It's possible once we've experienced it and it's impossible to go back to not craving that sense of belonging when the walk has been completed.

You have one life. It is time to really live it as you are meant to - richly, bravely and with daring.

Enjoy the journey.

About Amanda Candy

Having moved changing schools, homes and countries many times at a young age, Amanda learned to adapt to her new environments quickly. She spent years fitting into other people's lives never stopping to formulate her own identity. She became adept at being a chameleon. Whilst this was often exciting and interesting it didn't allow for her to develop her sense of self.

It was years before she created her own self by discovering her unique interests and abilities through much trial and deep inner learning.

These inherent and learned skills allow her to connect with people from all over the world from many varied backgrounds. She has an innate understanding of what people are going through, having been there herself.

It's been an extraordinary journey with one consistent gift: being resilient.

Honing her skills, she has created a deck of *Resilience Life Guidance Cards* that she is now teaching people to use enabling them to create the lives they are meant to live richly, bravely and with daring.

Currently living on the Sunshine Coast of Australia, Amanda runs workshops, does presentations and can be contacted at *www.amandacandy.com*

El Peregrino Cantante

Dan Mullins

I am a pilgrim, on the Camino and in life.

I'm a 51-year-old father of three and grandfather of two. *Soy un padre de tres hijos y tengo una nieta.*

I produce the top-rating radio show in Australia and I present a weekly segment called *The Bush Telegraph*. I've filed feature pieces from all over Australia, from the Gulf country to southwest Western Australia.

I've reported internationally from Beijing, England, Scotland - indeed it was my voice from the Palace of Westminster commemorating the Centenary of the outbreak of World War One in 2016 on radio stations right across Australia.

In terms of the Camino, I walked from Sahagun to Santiago in August 2016 (a gift from my family to mark my 50th birthday arriving in Santiago on the day of my 50th); and a year later I walked 1,000 kilometres from Lourdes in France to St Jean Pied de Port and along the Camino Francés to Santiago.

It was a long walk, but a very, very rewarding experience.

I also host *My Camino - the Podcast.*

Over the past two years I've interviewed young pilgrims, older pilgrims, people who walked as a couple, people who met on the Camino and became a couple, pilgrims who walked with their fathers, their mothers, their sons, their daughters.

They all tell a very different story - it may be their motivation; their discovery; their personal journey through pain; or their personal journey of the spirit. Everyone is different and so is every Camino.

I dragged out my Camino diary when putting together this article and it shed some light on what it means to be a pilgrim.

Under Day 32, 'O'Cebreiro to Samos' I wrote:

"Walking today in total euphoria ... magic scenery and Galicia starts to emerge before us. There's a theory that there are three stages to the Camino ... first you walk to emerge, then you find space on the Meseta and into Galicia you unwind completely.

"At times I feel the tribe unravelling ... then it comes together again at night ... it's like a human concertina – and it plays the most beautiful tune"

You walk the Camino, together alone.

You have to be a very good listener to be a good pilgrim. YOU never really grow unless you're prepared to listen and you'll HEAR more WHEN you listen. Not just from pilgrims - but also from Spain. Birdsong; cowbells; the crunching of gravel under your feet; laughter; conversation; encouragement; and most importantly love. Your temporary family.

I walked with seven other pilgrims - one of whom I went to school with as a boy. Bret Crosby and I traveled to Europe together and walked mostly apart joining one another each night at the albergue. I walked also with an Irish girl Ruth, a fiercely proud Welshman Lee, Jasper from Denmark, Lenny from Italy, Matthew from London and Igor, the Basque terrier from Bilbao.

We shared stories and songs, day after day and night after night - and when you're walking with someone, staying in the same places and sharing meals and washing your clothes together, you inevitably develop a very fierce friendship very quickly.

While others may come and go - as part of what I called our

Camino tribe, a much wider group of people - the Camino family felt as one. I arrived in Santiago de Compostela alongside all seven.

A pilgrim learns to understand you don't need all the baggage we carry in life. We don't need regrets; we don't need anger; we don't need turmoil. Easier said than done.

When I walked my first Camino in 2016 I walked alone. I didn't engage much with others - I was on a mission.

I decided I would dedicate each day of my journey to a five year period of my life and I'd try to remember everything. Where I lived, who I was friends with, people I hurt, people I helped, people who hurt me and those that helped me. Who I loved and who I didn't love.

Day One was years 1-5 - obviously I didn't remember much. Years 5-10, a bit more. Years 10-15 on Day Three I started to remember things I wanted - or needed to deal with.

I ended up in a sense tormenting myself for the rest of the trip. I thought of everything that needed dealing with for the first 50 years of my life. No regrets, no conflicts, no sadness, no failed ambitions, no failed opportunities. I dealt with it and left it all behind.

In my self-imposed madness I also left behind the opportunity to experience the wonders of the COMPANY of the Camino. I spent many nights on my own, I didn't engage with other pilgrims other than on the trail during the day, I was perhaps almost conducting a form of life's penance.

So when I returned in 2017 it was all about experiencing the best the Camino had to offer.

I carried a parlour guitar on my back and I had a policy that whenever anyone asked me to sing for them I would. I sang in old churches, in ruins, in pubs, in town squares, for pilgrim's birthdays, for their renewal, for their everything. It set me free, as a pilgrim, as a man and as a human.

In 2016, I spent most of the three weeks looking downward and inward. In 2017, I was determined to look up, to look back and to look forward.

As the Meseta loomed on my second Camino I was walking alone between Burgos and Hontanas, a journey of about 33 kms. I found myself about halfway through the day, just outside Hornillos del Camino, high up across the top of the plains.

I was walking alone, carrying my guitar, walking with poles and the gravel underfoot was crunching in time with the rhythm of the poles, creating a metronomic effect. I can still hear it today.

I often sing while I walk - I'm a musician by trade and still play at least twice a week in hotels, clubs and bars. I sing old songs, sort of crooning versions of songs and I find the solitude of the Camino draws the voice out of you.

So I started to sing:

Somewhere along the way ... somewhere along the way,
I hope you find what you're looking for,
somewhere along the way.

A lilting folksy melody, forming nicely with the lyric.

I remember thinking, "...who's song is that?" and "WHAT song is that?"

Again:

Somewhere along the way ... somewhere along the way,
I hope you find what you're looking for,
somewhere along the way.

Again, "WHAT song IS that?"

And then lyrics started to come to me:

El Camino roses, Santo Domingo crows
Believe you can, you're halfway there, seven bells to four

Now I was beginning to concentrate. I was intrigued. What was this song and where was it coming from?

More lyrics came.

Frighten off the horses, an old soul awakes
A lion's heart, an opening heart and a soul as old as slate

The chorus sat nicely …

Somewhere along the way, somewhere along the way,
I hope you find what you're looking for,
somewhere along the way

Another verse emerged …

Sellos on the soundboard, beneath a field of stars
La familia growing, crossing fields afar
Will you walk beside me, will you lead the way
Footsteps by the fountain, carry me away

And again the chorus …

Somewhere along the way, somewhere along the way,
I hope you find what you're looking for,
somewhere along the way

A middle eight rose.

How will I ever forget, the Spanish sunrise, the Spanish sunset

And another verse …

El peregrino cantante, fullness of the moon
Prayers beneath the arches, sunflowers in bloom
Words on parchment paper, fill an empty room
I hope this blessing, such as it is, finds you in full bloom

So here I was on the Camino with a song in my head –
a song I loved – and I wasn't sure if I would remember it,
whether I'd written it, was I dreaming it, it was bizarre. It had
never happened to me before. I sang it over and over – and the
lyrics were there each time. Word for word.

So I challenged myself to forget it – to let it go. I sang John Denver's *Annie's Song*:

You fill up my senses
Like a night in a forest

Every word, I sang the entire song. Then I waited.
Bang.
There it was…

El Camino roses, Santo Domingo crows
Believe you can, you're halfway there, seven bells to four

Unbelievable. I arrived in Hontanas about an hour later.

I promised myself before I left Sydney I would play my guitar and sing every time someone asked me. As I walked into town that afternoon, there was an albergue on the outskirts of the town, with a manicured garden, umbrellas and sun lounges.

A group of cyclists were sitting in the sun drinking beers. They called out to me "Hey, peregrino con la guitarra .... sing for us."

I remember pausing and saying to myself – really?

I said, OK.

So I walked back into the garden sat down and unpacked my guitar, they bought me a beer and I started to play. Tom Petty's *Free Fallin'.*

I stayed with them for about half an hour and then left to find somewhere to stay the night. I'd almost forgotten about the song and when I did think about it again, I was sure I would have forgotten it.

I checked into my albergue, had a shower, washed my clothes and grabbed my guitar before heading to the local café. I ordered a beer, and asked if they had any paper – all they had was a paper placemat. So I grabbed my pen and thought, "Well let's see if I can remember any of it".

I wrote out every word just as I'd sung it on the trail earlier that day.

Word for word.

The most astonishing thing is I didn't actually play the song. I didn't pick up the guitar and play it. I just knew how it went and how to play it. I folded up the paper and put it in my pocket.

Later that night, at a great dinner at our albergue to farewell our British brother Gary, I sang songs to wish him well. You've Got A Friend by Carol King, Bridge Over Troubled Water by Simon and Garfunkel.

Then I asked if anyone would mind if I sang a song I'd written that day. Everyone said go for it.

And I sang the song.

It brought the house down and I carry it with me every single day.

I has already brought enormous joy to hundreds of pilgrims and I'm sure it will continue to do so for many, many years to come.

I can't help thinking the Camino is an opportunity to grow.

I've interviewed people who have stepped outside their comfort zone, some of whom have reached unbelievable goals. They've outgrown themselves - and in some cases surprised themselves by what they were able to achieve.

Not only on the Camino, but once they've returned home to their everyday lives.

Because you've been an achiever. Because you've set yourself a goal and reached it - or maybe you didn't but gave it a red hot go. Because you stepped outside your comfort zone and decided to throw away all the pre-conceived conceptions you have of your own ability.

You proved to yourself you have more to give - more to live, more to share.

You proved to yourself you have an ability to grow; to live; to love; to be someone you never thought you COULD be.

Someone who is prepared to listen, to accept and to be quietly the person we all HOPE to be.

A pilgrim.

On the Camino and in life.

I hope YOU find what you're looking for, somewhere along the way.

About Dan Mullins

Dan Mullins is a Sydney-based singer/songwriter, radio producer, broadcaster and podcaster.

As a musician, playing 80 shows a year, Dan is a storyteller, a six-string troubador with soaring vocals and lilting melodies. He's played thousands of gigs, non-stop weekend after weekend, year after year, plying his trade in pubs and clubs the length and breadth of the country.

As a broadcaster he presents *The Bush Telegraph* weekly on the *Alan Jones Show* to 2GB in Sydney, 4BC in Brisbane and to 77 radio stations Australia-wide.

He is host of *My Camino - the Podcast*.

Dan wrote the song *Somewhere Along the Way (the Camino Song)* on the plains of Spain while walking 1,000 kilometres across Europe on the Camino de Santiago, the Way of St James, in the footsteps of millions of pilgrims before him. Their energy delivered the song straight to Dan's heart.

It's a yearning we all hold - to find what we're looking for.

Dan hopes to return to the Camino many times.

danmullinsmusic.net
Facebook Dan Mullins
Instagram @thesingingpilgrim
Twitter @2gbdanmullins
https://player.whooshkaa.com/shows/my-camino-the-podcast
Spotify My Camino

The End Is Nigh

Anne K Scott

I first saw this pilgrimage when I was in Swaziland, Africa in August 2012. I was sitting on an escarpment overlooking the ancient beginnings of civilisation. In the dusty haze a trail emerged laid out across scrubby, foreign land, a long, long walk leading all the way to the sea and, I imagined, a handsome sailor in a pea green boat. A romantic day dream.

I didn't realise then the many clues that would guide me to Saint Jean Pied de Port in France in October to join the *Camino Francés*. I did this walk for no other reason than it called me and I followed; curious about the rocky shore at the *End Of The World* and the reality of my metaphor. Could my sailor be some spiritual pilgrim in high-vis walking green or will it be the soul of my homeland Ireland on the distant horizon or perhaps something else all together? What colour is pea green anyway?

I arrive in Santiago de Compostela on my fortieth day of walking. I am continuing my pilgrimage to the lighthouse at Fisterra and then northwards to Muxia where the Virgin Mary purportedly appeared on a stone boat to encourage St. James in his efforts to evangelise the pagan Galicians.

The longer I walk the more entwined I have become with this land. I am blurred, not sure where my edges are any more.

I awake in the top bunk, alone, in this ugly albergue in Cee on my 45th day of walking.

The day before I lost Swiss Kevin. I first encountered Kevin two weeks earlier in the vineyards of El Bierzo. The work of harvesting over, the leaves are dying in a glory of red and

103

gold, dropping gently off the vines readying them for pruning. A darkening sky heralds rain as I am passing a make shift shed. I am glad of the invitation into the comfort of a big dilapidated armchair with a fizzing glass of homemade wine.

A speeding pilgrim passes by, a rain-caped Crusader, he disappears into the dusk on a mission. Not long later we break bread together at Albergue El Serbal y La Luna a magic place of stone and wood. After a rich lushness of garlic-coated roasted red peppers and ruby red Bierzo wine I am smoking cigarillos and we are star gazing the canvas of *La Via Lactea - The Milky Way*. For the next two weeks we are in rhythm. We rarely walk together but slide into a habit of supping Camino wine into the night and celebrate for two days in Santiago de Compostela. I missed his company last night in Cee.

Although I plan to continue up the coast to Muxia there is something about the lighthouse on Cabo Fisterra, today's destination, that has a finality to it.

Corcubion and Cee are kissing cousins, villages nuzzled up against each other, it is hard to see where one begins and the other ends but at some point jittery business is replaced by laid back indolence. I take the pretty medieval route through the town and up the shoulder to San Roque. It is a short 5 kms back to the seashore. The rhythm of walking calms my soul though the edginess of the end loiters in the back of my mind. I fancy breakfast facing out to sea, in a room with a picture window to frame the view. I pant hopefully up to and around the grand Hotel Playa de Estorde but this is off season and it is not open to cater for my whims.

I am enjoying the wildness of the sea but the day teeters on the edge of storminess. The vast dazzling white sands of Langosteria are dull and deadened by the sky. It is 10 kms now to Fisterra, in my imagination a romantic fishing town. I know there is a room for me there, white-walled and bright with achievement, waiting to embrace me with skin-stroking linen and jovial taverns cluttered with celebratory sea captains. The reality is more prosaic and I have to settle in glum resignation in a tidy, modern seafront cafe. All far too contemporary for me;

plasma TV, chrome tables and chairs, everyday encounters and business meetings. What the….?!

In denial I tramp the town with hope of THAT room and THAT linen. Hotel Naturaleza Mar da Ardora is a little rock of modern seaside architecture perched above the beach at the back of the town. It is *so* what I am looking for. And so not. It is closed, empty, hopeful. The owners show me around, I could have the whole place to myself but it would be pushing the budget and screaming out my aloneness. I opt instead for the hippy, run-down comfort of Albergue do Sol e da Lúa where my host mistakes my disgruntled humour as a judgement on his rooms and apologetically insists I can have a private room all to myself for little more than the price of a dorm bed. Even still all I want to do is get out of here, no soft linen to loll in or achievements to drink up.

I trudge for the light house, the final frontier, stolid and impassive, it's gimlet eye facing out to sea. The 0 km milestone, the museum, the peace pole and the fire pit accoutrements to it's primary role to warn of treacherous shores. My only companions here a Spanish couple who are walking around the coast of Spain for charity. A far more worthy cause than mine.

It is tradition for pilgrims to burn something in the fire pit below the lighthouse to represent the burdens they have let go of on the walk. I am holding on to every threadbare belonging and grizzly emotion. When I ask myself what is going on, I realise I am angry for not having the *right* kind of *pilgrim experience.*

The end of the known world is just not up to my standards. There is no sun, no champagne corks popping, no pals to high five, no coquilles St. Jacques on the beach and it is far too cold to delicately paddle my toes. I am on a craggy outcrop of the Atlantic on a stormy November day in a town that is just doing what it can do to get by off-season. There is no pea green boat, no handsome sailor-man, no one, just me.

I am drawn up a threadbare track towards the viewpoint of Monte Facho.

The sun streaks through the crowded clouds softening the stoney bulk of the lighthouse now below and illuminating the rugged beauty of the Costa da Morte northward. This isn't the end. I breathe. The struggle slowly seeps away. I am where I am, awake to the reality I am experiencing. I let it wash over me and around me. The tension drops. I realise I am beloved and that in truth I have loved this journey, my journey. I am smiling.

I text my long suffering parents, a little missive of joy skims across the grey Atlantic waters to the shore of Ireland and almost immediately I receive little tokens of congratulations by return.

I enjoy the boisterous gloomy walk up to the ruined remnants of the Ermita de San Guillerme to see the eponymous bed reknown for its miraculous powers of fertility.

This headland is layered with pagan and Christian ritual, an altar to the sun, a place where the spiritual and the material shake hands.

I am buffeted by the flailing curtains of this multi-verse

but I walk energised and exhilarated and find myself looking forward to the cheap warmth of the albergue.

It is a hive of activity when I get back and in repose, re-found, Swiss Kevin celebrating with hearty mugs of German pilgrims all set to wallow in beery inebriation. While I was looking down on the world stepping into my cloak of beloved, Kevin was at the lighthouse popping the bottle of bubbly we had talked about sharing. Ah well.

We head to dinner, seafood and a celebratory bottle of Albariño. A last night of Camino conversation before I retire to the luxury of my private room and Kevin to all night beer drinking with his German friends.

In the morning after an online flurry and a rumpled good-bye to a rather hung over Kevin I fumble my way up and over the scraggy edges of town. He returns to Switzerland and I am travelling onwards to Muxia.

The days at the dying of the year can be full of light and benign brightness or scratchy with rain and the furrowed brow of storm.

Today is one of the latter; the darkness of Thor's angry countenance lurks over the Costa Da Morte. There is a storm warning about. The south pointing finger of Cabo Fisterra behind me, I turn north and head out along the fractured exposed coastline. I am walking to Lires where I am booked into a Casa Rural for the night.

As I plateau I meet the boisterous salty cuffs of a wind that has careered unobstructed across the Atlantic, the air is electric with squall. It snatches at loose debris and gnaws the patchy forest for more bones for throwing. I catch glimpses of glorious beach and sea, stooks of hay splay anchored under the strange light of the scudding sky.

I am strangely at one with this raging energy, the creative flow of words swirl, forming into a shape that comes with the haunting twang of acoustic guitar. There is a symbiosis between us; the gale and I and we create a broken hearted love song. It cries copious, lachrymose sobs running rivulets down my face.

I am hunkered down
Licking yesterday's wounds
My howling heart
Racked and ruined
An angry sea boils up in me
Regrets of life's missing memories

Raw, broken, scarred
I whimper still
Feeling the ache
Of goodbye's bitter pill
I am wrung out, consumed
A ragged shadow of love's promise

My soul has opened wide
To connections I never knew
Across time and space
The principles are few
My spirit chose to dance with yours
In love, truth and unity

The debris of the storm
Is silent, lifeless dross
There is calm within my heart
I am through the wound of love and loss
Soul-cleansed and scrubbed alive
Core vibrations electrified

You came to me from nowhere near
You looked me in the eye
We shared a drink or two or three
I thought that I might cry
But instead I drank the joy
And saw you helped me fly

The church bells are ringing a death as I arrive at the pretty stone privacy of Casa Luz my stop for the night.

I had never been sick on this Camino, not a hint of a cold or the gyrations of a dicky tummy but in the morning when I wake I experience an angst and nervousness in my bowels. It didn't feel like anything I had eaten - more about the impending unknown; of life after the Camino.

This is my last day of walking. It is strange to experience my body crumple in fright about the expansiveness of life opening up again. I think I am excited but my reptilian brain is screaming *No!*

The remnants of rain are all around; sodden earth, dripping wires, saturated hedges, happy puddles but the rain clouds are gone and the sky wiped into a fresh powder blue. It is less than 15 kms to Muxia.

I am wrung out but this is a beautiful, white-washing day.

It's spirit nudges mine to soar a little and there is a rush of pleasure as I stride towards the end.

Even Miguel, the garrulous, Tigger-sprung policemen from San Sebastian, who latches on to me for this final stretch can't dampen my spirits.

Muxia is positively spruce and stylish compared to Fisterra, less world weary and more magical. A bubble of delight rises in me with the realisation that I have done it, I have walked the *Caminos Francés*, Fisterra and Muxia. I check into the business like and brightly friendly Albergue Bela Muxia. I love my private cubby hole of a bunk with personal locker, light and charging points. Super modern, super slick, the corporatisation of the Camino. I can't resist the t-shirt.

The following morning I have breakfast on my own assimilating this trip. I want to savour the last drops of it dripping slowly and honour it's closure.

A short walk from the town is the headland where the Virgin Mary appeared to a deflated Saint James struggling to convert the population of Fisterra from their pagan worship of the sun.

Mary's boat is still here, petrified on the headland below the imposing coastal Gothic style church of *Our Lady Of The Boat*. I was curious to see it.

Sure enough there are three huge stones one of which definitely looks like the upturned hull of the boat and another has a look of a sail. The third stone, supposedly the rudder, is a little less convincing.

I suppose it is no surprise that my original curiosity to follow the Camino to the sea was spurred by an imaginary sailor man. Muxia and Fisterra are fishing ports after all and where there be working boats, there be pleasure yachts and handsome sailors.

I had imagined an unfaltering step from terra firma onto the foot-worn warmth of an oak-planked deck and into the arms of a handsome sailor. I imagined us bobbing away into the ocean, a love story, like the *Owl and the Pussycat*.

Over lunch of whole baby squid, slathered in butter I muse the romance of my imagination. At the day's end the boat I left on was a modern day coach, a behemoth of a vehicle muscling its way through the narrow arteries of Galicia's rural rocky roads back to Santiago de Compostela.

And my companion? Miguel in his high tech fluorescent green walking jacket, both of us passengers back to life.

About Anne K Scott

Anne has 30+ years Information Technology experience as a programmer, designer and delivery manager.

As a manager of virtual teams challenged by time zones, language and cultural differences Anne specialised in bringing the best of diverse contributions and talents together to bring vision to reality.

In this increasingly fast moving world she found her spirit and resilience challenged. Facing questions about what was important to her she took time to study consciousness and personal leadership. Following her own guidance Anne walked her Caminos in 2012 embracing her love of walking and writing.

Anne has evolved a structure of working that blends her experience and studies with her love of exploration. She refers to herself as an *Imagination Technologist* as she works to create end results that can appear improbable if not impossible. Anne works with companies and individuals, who are willing to innovate, grow and are committed to realising their potential and the potential of their teams.

As part of the *On A Mission* coaching collaborative she is committed to the evolution of consciousness and creating a world of beautiful crazy possibilities. Anne speaks, teaches, coaches world-wide evolving and delivering innovation that matters.

www.crossingfrontiers.co.uk
LinkedIn: https://www.linkedin.com/in/annekscott/
Twitter: @annekscott
Facebook: https://www.facebook.com/ImaginationTechnologist/

Choosing The Camino Inglés

Susan Jagannath

More people have heard of the *Camino Francés* than of the less popular *Camino Inglés,* or English Way, of St. James. The *Camino Inglés* is an authentic pilgrimage route taken by English and Northern European pilgrims during the middle ages, who came by sea from their homelands to La Coruña or Ferrol, and then walked to Santiago. Santiago de Compostela is about 60 kms from La Coruña, and 120 kms from Ferrol.

I had been longing to do the *Camino Francés* for over ten years – and mostly it was the time needed that was the barrier. I came across the *Camino Inglés,* a different one from the famous *Camino Francés,* and it was only a week long.

If you think you are too old, too unfit, too far away or too busy for the *Camino Francés,* then this is definitely the Camino for you. And if you do want to do the *Camino Francés* one day, this is for you, too. You will probably fall in love with Spain and want to come back!

Don't wait to do the Camino. There's a little one that you can do right now, so stop waiting and start walking! BUT, identify why you are doing the Camino.

The *Camino Ingles* is such a short one and so well marked that you do not really need a step-by-step guide on the route. Just follow the markers!

What should you do if you can't walk that much?

Start by walking as much as you can every day, and solutions will present themselves. But remember that you should talk to your doctor before starting any training, including walking. In fact, you can be a grandparent and you can take your grandkids with you as well! I met a woman with only 6% vision and deaf in one ear, who had forgotten her white cane at home, and still completed the walk!

Find the right footwear and break them in before you start your Camino. Walk in the boots during training so that any problems can be fixed before you go. For example, I found my feet were hurting too much, and it felt like I was coming up with shin splints or tendonitis. A visit to the podiatrist and a pair of orthotics fixed that in a day or so, and I was able to continue training.

The *preparation phase* is a good opportunity to get fit.

The best way to do this is to fix your nutrition. You will find that the extra exercise actually curbs your appetite and cravings. If you haven't been supplementing, this is the time to start with good quality vitamins and supplements. We ate a lot of high-quality protein, with good fats and minimal carbs.

But this is not a journey about shedding weight. We cut out all sugar, cut down on alcohol and caffeine, and increased our intake of proteins and salad. It's amazing how healthy you eat when you have a physical and mental goal clear in your head! I was going to enjoy the chocolate and churros and wine on the trail, so I was going to get fit and shed some weight beforehand.

Don't let a lack of Spanish deter you.

While you cannot become fluent in a week, you can use a few words and phrases to manage. Download a Spanish app or translator onto your phone and spend some time each day practicing a few words. Take a tiny notebook and write down some phrases; if you need glasses, write the phrases down large using a marker pen. Or just use a single word with an upward inflection to indicate a question.

It is safe to walk the *Camino Inglés*. Take care when walking along muddy paths, as stepping stones can sometimes be slippery.

Carry snacks and water, though you can refill water at the many fuentes along the way.

Decide if you are going to carry a backpack or not.

Be practical here: if it's going to be a factor in preventing you from doing the Camino, don't hesitate in getting it ported every day.

We stayed in one albergue, in Neda, it was a basic albergue with sweeping river views and it was totally empty. We stayed in all types of accommodations and enjoyed the experience! The albergue in Bruma is on the ancient medieval route where the two Caminos from La Coruña and Ferrol meet.

The end of Day 2 left me both exhausted and exhilarated, as the trek took me up into hilly slopes forested with eucalyptus and then down to clean, sandy beaches.

In Pontedeume I wandered around the the medieval centre of town before preparing for Day 3 with a good sleep.

On Day 3, I was nearing the middle of the journey with a number of short climbs and descents all the way into the walled, medieval town of Betanzos. We hadn't had a chance to actually enter a church, because they were closed, but the Church of San Francisco made up for that.

On Day 4, I reached the spot where the two pilgrim routes from Ferrol and La Coruña meet, incontrovertible evidence that you are walking in the footsteps of millions of pilgrims from over a thousand years. Bruma is where the two ancient pilgrim routes meet, so it is well-documented as the medieval hospice for pilgrims.

On Day 5, the penultimate day I felt a mixture of relief and the beginning of a strange sadness, and started wondering what I'd learned or gained.

To reach Siguiero, we walked at least 27 kms today. The joy of the Camino is connecting back to the simplest but most profound of pleasures that almost classifies as sheer joy: good food, cold water and clean clothes.

I contemplated how far I'd come and how close I was to my goal! Five days ago I started out on my first Camino, 100+ kms

MY CAMINO WALK #1

by foot. I am not the same person who caught the flight from home.

On Day 6, I entered Santiago and the cathedral and my journey ended, but reaching my goal inspired me in all areas of your life, and to larger and other goals.

Buen Camino!

You've finished the course, achieved your goal and got your compostela. You're now a *certified pilgrim*, and more importantly, you know you can do anything you decide to, as you have proof that you have succeeded. In Latin.

I hate to add a disclaimer, but here it is. This book is based on my personal experience, and while I have checked and rechecked details, you are responsible for your own health and happiness on the Camino.

Buen Camino!

About the Susan Jagannath

Susan successfully combines a passion for reading, a love of writing and a fascination for technology, to create a career in technical writing.

With over 50 technical manuals (not) to her name, *RTFM* could be the motto for her life; but she never lets the *"No one ever reads the Manual"* myth stop her from enjoying her work as a technical author.

As an army brat, her childhood included seven different schools, three universities and a couple of emergency evacuations from conflict zones.

Travel and adventure were normal. She believes in seizing every opportunity to have a new adventure.

Whether it's camping on the beach in Australia, trekking in the Himalayas, kayaking in Queensland, whitewater rafting down the Ganges, or walking the Camino in Spain, her philosophy is to pack it into one or two weeks to create memories for a lifetime, (and disconnect from television and computer games, including *Pokemon Go*).

Susan is now on her next adventure; writing books that are not technical manuals, training to be an awesome grandmother, and planning her next getaway.

If you are interested in finding out more about Susan Jagannath's books, and getting some freebies, you can check it out at *www.susanjagannath.com*

"Thank you for reading The Camino Inglés! I hope it makes your Camino a reality and you have wonderful adventures on the Way. If you enjoyed this book, please leave a review on Amazon."

My One Camino ... In Two Years

Paul ter Wal

In September 2012, I decided to go walk the Camino. I didn't have a monumental reason to do so, but I wanted to experience how it would be to go out of my comfort zone, by being away for 30 days in a different environment and without any device. Another reason was to find out whether I could walk a distance like this, alone.

As I'm a long distance walker, I love to walk in the High Sauerland, West-Germany, I prepared myself in the normal way. Using older shoes, that had made hundreds of kilometres and with a rucksack, that had been around for a longer time.

I checked the internet on what to bring and then decided that because my start would be on Eastern Sunday, March 30, 2013, I would bring some extra warm clothes with me. Finally, my rucksack was loaded with 12 kilos of gear.

I went by train van Amsterdam to Paris and from Paris to Biarritz, France. There I found out that I had lost my small mobile phone. I was advised to buy one in Pamplona with a Spanish SIM card.

The next morning I went by diesel train to Saint Jean Pied de Port. From the train station a group of walkers went into the town and I just followed them into the town. There I found my hostel for the first night, owned by Dutch people, just across the street of the *Pilgrim* office. A good environment to start the Camino. The first day we crossed the Pyrenees to Roncesvalles.

On Day 3, I walked with some other Dutch and Danish walkers to Pamplona.

Until then all went well, although we had all kinds of weather in those first days: snow, rain, sun, heat and cold.

Close to Pamplona, we had to walk a side way because of an accident on the road. There I stepped into a mud hole and fell down. At first I couldn't get up. My right leg was hurting. Finally, one of the pilgrims pulled me up, holding my rucksack. Result of this fall: two torn ankle ligaments. We didn't know it by then so, we taped the ankle and I took some pills to go on.

In Pamplona, I went to see a physiotherapist and he said I could walk on: nothing was broken, and could take some *Ibuprofen* to kill the pain. After this visit and me buying a phone, I took a hotel to rest and to wash all my stuff.

In this hotel I had the chance to take a look at all the stuff that I needed or not. I noticed that some of the stuff I was carrying, was still unused. Also, some cloths were especially for the cold weather and I didn't think I would use them anymore. So, I took two kilos of gear out of my rucksack and send it home by post, where it arrived long after I was back home.

The next morning, I just restarted and walked out of Pamplona on April 2, 2013. I had enough *Ibuprofen* to go on and keep walking. Walking with two kilos less helped me very much. It felt like my rucksack was much lighter than before and it helped me to go even with my leg hurting. I know now that carrying that extra two kilos would have stopped me earlier from finishing the Camino: it's all about your carrying capacity in life.

It all went well until April 13, 2018. I was close to Fromista, when I felt ill.

Coming from Castrojerez, you have to climb a steep mountain; it's like a wall. On top of this cliff, I was so tired that I had to take a long break at the nearest bar.

As I sat there drinking a tea (that means that I'm really sick, otherwise I would have taken a coffee), a Spanish walker approached me and asked me how I was feeling, because I was completely pale. I told him the story of the mud hole and that my stomach was hurting, I think because of the *Ibuprofen*.

He then said he would go and ask a friend of his in Boadilla del Camino, in En El Camino Albergue to take care of me when I arrived. Another guy who was sitting there with him said he would walk with me and take care of me on the way to Boadilla. That man, Chris, told me his life story; how he left his family just after his daughter was born: his wife kicked him out of the house because he was drunk and violent. He travelled around the world walking and working. And that he hadn't seen his daughter for 13 years. So, he decided to go to Santiago and ask for forgiveness.

This companion and his story helped me to get to the albergue. And there the friend was standing in the doorway waiting for me. And although they were closed at that moment, he and his lovely family took care of me. They gave me a cup of tea, helped me with my shoes and my rucksack; I could take a long shower and they washed my clothes.

Now, this albergue is amazing: it's like in the sixties, with a lot of love, flowers and just nice people. But I didn't notice it that Saturday, I was too sick.

That evening the family took me to Carrion de los Condes to the *Pilgrim's Clinique*. There, the doctors decided that I had to stop my Camino and go home.

Of course, I was very disappointed and had to cry. I called my wife to tell her that I was forced to stop and that I would get home in a few days.

When I got back in the albergue, my rucksack and shoes were gone. The family didn't want me to leave early in the morning instead of staying and prepare my return home.

That morning Chris came to see me and he asked what the doctors said. He felt sorry for me that I had to stop. Then he told me that he had dreamed that night that his daughter was calling him to come home. And he told me that he would stop drinking and wanted to go home and be with his daughter.

Months later I received an email from Chris; he was sober and was living close to his daughter. This is one of the miracles of the Camino.

That Sun(ny)day I stayed at the alberque, they got the right medication for me and I arranged to go to Barcelona by train on Monday and take a plane home on Tuesday. And so I did.

In Barcelona, I felt much better already, I think because of all the medicine I had taken instead of the *Ibuprofen,* that had upset my stomach very bad. That was a good lesson: never have *Ibuprofen* without protective medicine for your stomach.

On Tuesday afternoon I arrived by train in my hometown Zwolle; my wife and son were waiting for me. They expected to see a very ill man, but I felt so much better already.

The next morning, I went to the physiotherapist and there I learned that my injury was so bad that I could have been in pain for a long time: I hadn't been listening well enough to my body during the walk.

The next year, April 13 2014, I was back in the *same* alberque on the *same* date, to restart and finish my Camino. The son who took care of me a year before, saw me and put his hand on his tummy and asked, *are you well again?* He still remembered me after a whole year. Isn't that amazing?

So, on my *Pilgrim's Passport* you will find two stamps of the same location with almost the same date April 13: in 2013 and in 2014.

The next two weeks, I walked the rest of my Camino.

I arrived in Leon on Good Friday and witnessed all the wonderful processions during the afternoon and the evening. This was so intense and spiritual.

The last day, April 27, 2014, I walked more kilometres than I planned. Close to the airport of Santiago and still 12 kilometres away from the centre, I met a Scottish biker who offered me a whisky when I would meet him at 6pm on the main square of Santiago. This gave me a good feeling to finish that day even when I was tired.

That afternoon, I finished my Camino.

I felt strange because a long and intense trip had come to an end. It was great to be on the square and going into the Cathedral with the Botafumeiro, but I felt sad.

Maybe, you know that feeling. I received two Compostelas: one from the *Pilgrims office* and one from the *Benedictines*.

That evening I enjoyed a lovely meal and talk with the biker. The next days, other pilgrims I met during this two weeks would finish their Camino and we had a great closing evening before every one went his own way.

On Wednesday, I left as well, promising myself to walk the Camino gain some day.

For me, this Camino, although I walked in two years, still feels like one Camino.

My take-away of my Camino is: You may walk the Camino alone, but you won't be alone on the Camino, ever.

About Paul ter Wal LLM, CSP, FPSA

Paul ter Wal is a professional speaker and consultant, who took four weeks out over two years to walk his Camino.

His main activities involve developing and co-implementing new accountability, employee engagement and absence leave concepts, in which both internal and external interpretations are given to the employer's desired approach for prevention, labour care, intervention and re-integration: the vitality-approach.

He is speaking about employee engagement and accountability for companies, public seminars; he's also an in-demand MC for conventions on his topic.

https://www.linkedin.com/in/paulterwal/

https://www.paulterwal.com

How to Walk the Camino

Matt Wright

"It's easy – you just Walk, Eat, Sleep, Repeat."

This was the mantra we learned on the last night of walking our first Camino — the *Camino Francés* — over a communal dinner in a lovely little albergue in the hamlet of St Irène.

It was one of those special moments, just like you see in the movies; many different nationalities gathered around a long table, breaking bread, drinking wine, and excitedly swapping stories, all the more so because we were all just one day's walk from our destination — Santiago de Compostela.

It's a mantra which I've often pondered upon since, one which reduces life to its most elemental, stripping back the layers of complexity from our everyday lives.

Whilst not profoundly religious myself and having found the word *pilgrim* rather off-putting initially, (envisaging scores of chanting walkers and daily group prayer sessions) these four words — *Walk, Eat, Sleep, Repeat* — summed up the simplicity of the Camino for me, and why so many people come back to walk it again and again.

I guess you could call it therapy for the soul, or maybe the Camino is just a different type of religion?

However, before you arrive at this epiphany, there is a lot to go through beforehand, so here are a few (hopefully) helpful tips and pieces of experience picked up along the way.

Training

For those who swear by the saying *Quality over Quantity*, I'm afraid that this maxim doesn't apply to the Camino — it should read *Quality AND Quantity*.

It's the repetitive and unrelenting nature of the Camino that gets to people and breaks down bodies, with feet taking the most punishment. For a detailed explanation of the preparation we undertook, please feel free to browse our blog:

*http://www.jackiemattadventures.com/
preparation-camino-Francés/*

A typical Camino routine

It's as much mental as physical once on the Camino, so you need to develop a routine. Some people are early risers, some are late (although this is more of a challenge in a shared dorm with a check-out time of 8am), some like the heat, some don't … so find whatever works best for you. Our routine for the *Camino Francés* (May-15) was as follows:

- **6:45am** – Aim to start walking.
- **8:00am** – Breakfast after at least 5km, very rarely earlier, we'd sometimes walk up to 10kms which allowed us to break the day up into segments. So if we'd pretend that the day hadn't yet started until we'd had breakfast, so it was already at least 5kms magically shorter than planned.
- **11:30am** – Aim to have done a 10km stint before stopping for our mid-morning break. Again, this wasn't a hard and fast rule and depended upon the quality of cafés and the scenery that we passed — remember, you've always got time to stop and smell the flowers!
- **12:00 noon** – *'21km by 12'* was one of our mantras. 21kms represents a half-marathon, so we would visualise a race which we'd run previously and aim to be over the finish line by 12:00 (this also helped when

counting down the kilometres to 21 kms). This meant that for a 30 km-walking day, we would already be about two thirds of the way through before we'd consider stopping for lunch.

Changing routines for the Camino Portugués and Camino del Norte

When we tried to re-enact this routine for the *Camino Portugués* (Mar-16) it proved rather difficult owing to the lack of stopping options, especially on the less popular Lisbon – Porto leg. This meant we had to become more flexible — we couldn't rely upon a café being open or available for breakfast and had to plan our lunch stops more carefully as well.

Likewise for the *Camino del Norte* (Jun-17), especially during the initial stages when we found that café stops were few and far between. For coastal Caminos, it's worth remembering that a number of establishments close out-of-season, so you do need to shop and pack up in advance — a small cooler bag is a very useful item to have with you to store sandwiches and fruit.

Ten practical tips 'n tricks for the Camino

Air your boots upside down

- It's more effective = less moisture in the sole.
- Easier to find on communal boot racks first thing in the morning.
- If wet/damp, stuff with scrunched up newspaper.

Experiment with different boot lacing patterns

- Over 90% of people never re-lace their shoes from the 'traditional' cross lace format.
- Use the heel lock hole — it's there for a reason …just Google *heel lock* and you'll see!
- *https://www.locklaces.com/blogs/resources/ how-to-tie-a-heel-lock*
- Use vertical lacing to relieve mid-foot pressure and wrap-arounds for extra tension.

Mark your Poles

- You should be able to hold them normally with your elbows bent at 90°.
- Wrap some tape round the pole to mark your *normal* flat walking level.
- This also helps you to identify your poles when placed in a communal bin in the albergue.

Colour-coded stuff sacks

- Good ones are fully waterproof, whereas rucksacks generally aren't. Also, if you have a water bladder in your rucksack which leaks, you'll be protected (it happens … quite a lot!)
- Different colours = different uses. This is invaluable at *silly* o'clock in the morning when leaving dormitories; e.g. I used a small red one for my dirty laundry, which also contained travel wash and clothes pegs, so all my washing stuff was always in one place and ready to go.

Tie shoe laces onto zips

- Shoe laces can break, especially in wet/damp weather.
- Wrap a spare shoe lace around one of the zips on the side pocket of your rucksack.
- If it's a well-used side pocket (say for toiletries) then it makes it even easier to locate in the dark.

Emergency money holder

- You can buy a small cylinder which fits onto a zip (preferably the top pocket so it doesn't dangle about too much).
- It is capable of taking one rolled-up €20 note for emergencies.
- It also makes your top zip easier to find, which is where you put your *easy access* items.

Two pairs of exactly the same walking shorts

- I used to keep the same things in the same pockets of my walking shorts; e.g. Brierley guide bottom left thigh pocket, credencial in bottom right…etc.
- Having another identical pair, in a different colour, enabled me to swap stuff over from my dirty shorts without losing anything in the process.

Choose a liner or a micro sleeping bag – not both

- Unless you're walking in the depths of winter, you don't need a big sleeping bag.
- We initially started off with big 1.5kg bags which hung and swung beneath our rucksacks, but massively downsized on our second trip to tiny 600g sleeping bags from Decathlon *(www.decathlon.co.uk)* — so much lighter and they could fit inside our rucksacks.

Rubber pole tips

- If you're doing a lot of road walking, the clickety-clack of metal walking pole tips can get rather annoying, as well as being less effective (slippery on asphalt!)
- *https://caminoways.com/walking-poles*
- Rubber pole tips give you some bounce on hard surfaces and provide you with more 'upright' security.
- Buy them in advance – we found it difficult to find replacements en route.

Buy two credencials before you set off (or buy extra credencials en route whenever you can)

- Credencials are available in bigger cities (alternative starting points) and some albergues, but you can guarantee that when you're running out of space, you won't find one! *https://caminoways.com/walking-the-camino-passports-certificates-compostelas*
- Since you can stamp your credencial at restaurants/bars along the way (not just for accommodation), they can fill up quickly.

- Far better to stamp at every opportunity and have an attractive visual reminder of the route you walked and where you stopped, than having to skimp to save spaces.

Get out that and enjoy life!

Don't wait until you have a free five-week window to walk a Camino — you don't have to do it all in one go! We walked a three-week section from St Jean to Léon (May-15), which left us a shorter section from Léon to Santiago (Sep-15) to complete the *Camino Francés*. This left us relatively fresh and with time to visit Finisterre and walk from there to Muxia, which was probably one of the magical parts of our entire Camino. So by rushing, your risk missing what's under your nose.

We experienced so many wonderful highs (and some fairly dramatic lows!) over the course of our three Caminos, which we documented on a day-by-day basis on our website blog.

It's so difficult to choose the highlights from well over 1,000 miles of walking, but the following five examples should provide some sort of context:

Night out in Burgos (Day 11, Camino Francés)

Part of the joy of the Camino is meeting people; some you drift across again and again on a daily basis, some you meet once and then never again. So, it was a great experience to be able to arrange to hook up in advance with some of the firm friends we made in first fortnight of our virgin Camino, in the knowledge that some would be leaving soon afterwards.

Burgos is a fantastic jewel of a city, with an amazing cathedral, open plazas and a very buzzing nightlife, and even though we were extremely early by Spanish standards (who rarely eat before 9pm) we enjoyed a memorable evening tapas bar-crawling our way through the city centre before bidding tearful farewells.

Coastal walk, Finisterre - Lires (Day 28, Camino Francés)

After the increasingly commercialised hustle and bustle of the last 100km, when tour groups start to dominate and the Camino loses some of its early mellow appeal, it was so refreshing to travel out to Finisterre, see the proper end of the Camino, and then spend two relaxed days walking to Muxia which many people regard as the true spiritual destination. The smell of the pine forests that hug the coastline, mixed with sea-salt air and the absolute solitude were just the antidote we needed to round off our Camino.

Sodden and freezing, Albergaria a-Velha (Day 11, Camino Portugués)

This was one of those low Camino days, which started off poorly and got steadily worse as the day went on, leaving us stranded on a Sunday (when everything closes in Portugal) in a non-descript modern town with no amenities and a freezing bunkhouse room (marble is fine for the summer heat, but not for the spring chill!)

Refreshed cycling, Porto (Day 13, Camino Portugués)

However, as so often is the case, dramatic lows are soon followed by wonderful highs. We left Albergaria and made it to Porto where we had a day off – the sun shone, we hired bicycles and cycled up the coast to Mostinhos where we lay on the beach, sat on the beachside BBQ restaurants drinking cold vinho verde out of pitchers whilst eating grilled seafood which had been almost literally thrown across the road by the fishermen opposite.

A day of two halves, Laredo – Guemes (Day 9, Camino del Norte)

It's not often you get to start your day's walking with ferry ride over a crystal blue bay, then walk barefoot along miles of beach until lunchtime. This is how our day started when walking out of Laredo, and after a leisurely sunbathing break on the beach at Noja we decided to keep Spanish time and have a proper sit-down three-course set menu lunch.

We had thought we had only 10 kms to go, but managed to get slightly lost (must have been the rosé at lunchtime) and ended up walking almost 20 kms further in the blazing heat, arriving at Guemes Monastery just in time for the compulsory 45-minute pre-dinner speech by the old pastor.

In summary

These Caminos have given us so many wonderful memories, it almost feels like a privilege being allowed to walk them and join part of a unique, ever-changing community. If you do one thing in your lives, it should be to walk a Camino, to embrace its highs and lows, and to find some peace within yourself … *Walk, Eat, Sleep, Repeat* … it's that simple.

About Matt Wright

Matt Wright is a freelance copywriter who, over the last three years, has walked the *Caminos Francés, Portugués* and *del Norte.*

Having lived abroad extensively, both whilst growing up and throughout his working career, Matt speaks Spanish, French, and Dutch, so it should come as no surprise that travel and exploration have become such a passion.

Matt writes extensively through his company *Nobleword* for online (websites, blogs, newsletters), hard copy (articles, customer research), and prospective authors (proofreading, copyediting, ghostwriting).

linkedin.com/in/matt-noble-wright-52915861
www.nobleword.co.uk
Camino blogs: www.jackiemattadventures.com

Finding My Tribe On The Camino

Janet Russell

I stepped onto the worn cobbled street of St Jean Pied de Port, took a deep breath and realised I was actually doing it. It was mid September, almost two years to the day since my brother had taken these same first steps. Inspired back then by his Camino journey and the freedom and physical challenge such a long walk offered, the reality of me doing it would be many years away.

Or so I thought.

I had responsibilities like parenting, marriage and a full-on corporate role that made taking several weeks out for *me time* a far off dream. Yet within a year both my marriage and my job had dramatically imploded. It was a stormy period of change.

A year later, encouraged by my daughter and a new partner who had walked the Camino and wanted to do it again, I took those first memorable steps in St Jean Pied de Port and felt a little like a hobbit leaving the Shire on an unknown quest.

My partner and I were moderately fit. We had spent the past two weeks doing short hikes in the picturesque Basque region of southern France. Excited as I was to be finally on the *Camino Francés,* that first morning was tough.

Adjusting to the weight of my pack - which was relatively light at 6.7kg - I paused every 100 metres in some steep sections, catching my breath and gulping water under an endless blue sky.

There were fewer than 20 pilgrims on the road that morning. I was not the only one panting and pausing on the winding climb.

The valley views of quaint Basque villages receding below us were postcard perfect.

As sunscreen ran in uncomfortable rivulets down my neck, the magical lure of the Camino pulled me forward. My walking poles were welcome extra limbs as I levered my legs onwards up the dusty gravel road. I was so relieved when our first night's lodging at Orisson came into sight.

Many walkers spurn the idea of staying at Refuge Orisson, because it is only 8 kms from St Jean Pied de Port. Bookings at Orisson often need to be made months in advance. Instead, most peregrinos do a long 25 km+ hike up the hills, cresting the Pyrenees and crossing into Spain to sleep at Roncesvalles.

I didn't realise it then, but staying at Orisson was a gift that would shape my whole Camino experience. Many of the peregrinos I met at Orisson would become part of my daily landscape, coming clearer into focus with each shared walk, meal, or lodging.

The Camino stories I'd read mostly spoke about it being a solo pilgrimage, allowing time for introspection and finding yourself. This conjured up images of quiet, contemplative walking leading to a serene state of knowing more about yourself by journey's end. Being a good introvert, this inner journey held much appeal. However, the opportunity to meet new people, to connect, to be curious about their journeys and share stories, was a much stronger pull.

This is how I wanted to walk my Camino and staying at Orisson was the perfect entrée.

That first night maybe 35-40 peregrinos sat down at long tables for dinner. A fascinating mix of ages, nationalities, solo walkers, couples and groups of friends. Polite chatter filled the large room.

During dinner the Orisson hosts asked us to introduce ourselves to the whole group, and, if we felt like it, to share the reason for our walk.

Such diverse introductions, some disclosure, and some sharing little more than their names. Not everyone was walking the full distance as they had limited time. A few had walked the Camino more than once.

By last drinks, acquaintances were forming, and walking plans shared. That evening was the beginning of my Camino tribe.

Next morning, the rain that had loudly blown in overnight eased to a drizzle with a thick fog shrouding the Pyrenees.

Layered in waterproof jackets, my partner and I were amongst the last to leave Orisson. We were fast walkers and within minutes caught up to those who had left earlier; the familiarity of the previous evening making for easy small talk.

With the constant clanging of cow bells guiding us ever upwards through the rain and mist, we chatted with almost everyone we came across. The talk of that day was mostly about protecting our feet, with a couple of pilgrims already experiencing blisters. Feet, ankles and knees need respect to walk 15kms-30kms+ each day.

My partner had suffered on his first Camino with foot problems until a helpful refugio owner showed him how to adjust his boot laces to suit downhill walking so the toes weren't pushing forward into the toe box; a common cause of blood blisters. High on the misty mountain, he happily shared this knowledge with two very grateful Irish women, re-lacing their boots for the slippery descent.

I didn't wait to get blisters or sore spots on my feet. Each morning I applied a thick piece of sticking plaster to my heels and across the balls of both feet. I then interwove New Zealand hiking wool between my toes, put on my socks and carefully laced my boots for the conditions expected that day.

Unlike many horror feet stories, I suffered nothing more than small blisters on my little toes and some chafing around the top of my boots on warmer days.

By the time we checked into the old monastery at Roncesvalles we had a dinner date in the village with eight others, including the delightful Irish women and a wonderful trio from Seattle. This group would become the early core of my Camino tribe, attracting and embracing others like a magnet as the days rolled on.

The youngest member of our tribe was a flame haired 26-year old from the Lake District in England, who was initially nervous about walking by herself. Our oldest member, from New Jersey in the USA, had just turned 80: he was an experienced hiker and serial Camino pilgrim.

Some days we walked with one or more of our tribe, shared a meal or found ourselves staying in the same albergue. Equally, days could pass until we reconnected, usually with shouts, hugs and much bonhomie as we reunited like old friends. Very little was planned, but when you are all walking at a similar pace on the same path, the opportunities to connect are constant.

My partner and I enjoyed finding places for our tribe to meet. Via word of mouth we would sometimes end up with 10-15 pilgrims gathering for an evening drink or a meal in some memorable setting.

One such night we shared wine on long tables outside the majestic Café Iruna in Pamplona. It was a United Nations cocktail of languages and nationalities: Fins, Swedes, Koreans, Australians, Israelis, Germans, Canadians, Americans, Irish, English and more. A happy, noisy group of peregrinos finding its way.

Other days brought birthday celebrations, shared picnic lunches, quick coffee stops, evening tapas, and farewell meals for those who were not walking all the way to Santiago.

Conversations deepened amongst some of our tribe. We told our heart stories, raw and intimate, that became part of what we left on the path as our feet swelled and burned under the weight of all we carried.

I still hold close the teary secrets, fears, longings and regrets entrusted to me and the Camino.

In the moments and days when it was just my partner and I walking together, the intimacy of the raw conversations we had with others, helped us to share more of our own heart stories. Stories of loss, love, grief, families and our hopes for a future together. Some days we walked in a beautiful shared silence, grateful for the moment, or we listened to music and podcasts and poetry.

I discovered the recordings of Irish poet, author and priest John O'Donohue. I walked for hours listening to his mellifluous voice and sage words.

The Camino is a different experience for everyone but I came away with two observations.

Firstly, the attraction of the Camino for many is about connecting with yourself – body, head and heart.

Secondly, it's about connecting with others. Or, how we choose to disconnect or keep a distance from others. In the way we connect or fail to connect with others, it can tell us so much about ourselves, not all of which is pretty.

Many personal stories I've read about the Camino focus on how much it can positively change your life. This isn't always so.

I know pilgrims who shattered old friendships, and others who found the physical challenge too much and had to stop walking. I thought I would spend most of my days in my own head or talking with my partner. By consciously choosing to be part of a very sociable tribe, I gained so much more from the whole experience, including several wonderful friendships.

My partner and I will soon walk another Camino, this time starting in Portugal. We hope to once again find a tribe with whom to share the journey. I'm as excited about this next walk as I was that first day on the cobbled streets of St Jean Pied de Port.

Buen Camino!

About Janet Russell

Janet is a mother, management educator and executive coach based in Melbourne, Australia.

In September 2015, Janet and her partner Larry walked the *Camino Francés* route.

They are currently planning their next Camino walk, this time starting in Portugal.

http://linkedin.com/in/janet-russell-a270573

The Camino of Smiles

Sarah Hewitt Rippon

There are a myriad of good reasons for walking the Camino but mine were simple: to prove to myself that turning 50 was the beginning of a new adventure; that it was possible to de-sensitise myself and sleep with a roomful of strangers for a month; that I could carry my essentials in a backpack and walk 700kms whilst retaining a sense of humour at all times.

We had arrived in Portugal at the end of September 2017 and walked the tranquil but challenging Portuguese Camino from Porto to Santiago in ten days. On reaching Santiago, our legs were still fresh so we decided to head east and walk the *Camino Francés ... in reverse.*

What follow are daily anecdotes of quite possibly the best birthday gift ever!

October 10, 2017 Villanova da Arousa - Santiago

A fresh river ride to Padrón, a 25 km respite for the feet, an excitable local who refused to sell us cafe grande in a mug (in a cup only, si!), a belated birthday sherry from the albergue owner in Milledoura, a lovely walk and talk to a Portuguese osteopath with a Yorkshire accent and then the anticipated entrance into Santiago.

Mixed feelings as I wondered if I should attend the mass with the masses, and how many people had found the answers they were looking for, healed a broken heart, overcome blisters and bruised feet and made it to the final destination of millions of pilgrims. The city was literally heaving as peregrinos queued for 2-3 hours for their compostelas. The queues were too long, so we decided to sit and cheer in the limping and hobbling peregrinos.

Around sunset and after much debate and advice, we got on the road, direction Lugo and became *Peregrinos Regresso*.

And boy, did we confuse the tide pouring into Santiago.

The competitive youngsters got quite upset, shouting *wrong way!*, the solo walkers asked politely if they were going the right way but most stared and quickly checked their maps and the direction of the yellow arrows.

Little did they realise that we were using them to show us the way as the *Camino Regresso* is not easy when the yellow arrows only point one way.

Just outside Santiago - O Pino

The day started with a 7am eviction in the pitch dark by the fierce, mop-wielding albergue owner. Cleaning wet bathroom floors is a thankless task but most albergues provide a mop for peregrinos to clean up after themselves.

The morning air was fresh and we wondered if we should rather be on a sun-kissed beach, sipping cocktails and lying around. But the *Camino Regresso* was in full swing and the promise of walking most of the *Camino Francés* in reverse in beautiful Galicia was beckoning. We were like salmons swimming upstream and the strange looks and comments continued.

We found an abandoned house and the company of a neglected stallion for our lunchtime picnic. By 6pm, aching feet and no albergues in sight for another two hours when our guardian angel arrived in a taxi and offered us accommodation at his pension. A peaceful night at last!

Pino - Ribadiso

On several occasions we had looked at our backpacks and wondered what to leave behind but now the weather was changing, the layers were appreciated! Another fun day as we walked against the flow of pilgrims, read the *Wall of Wise Words* and received the biggest slice of pizza by a kind man seconding a Spanish cycling team.

A post on the Camino blog caught my eye before we left - does one lose weight on the Camino? In my experience the answer was definitely not as one is hungrier than a caterpillar and there are so many new delicious looking and tasting delicacies to try.

A Spanish bank holiday and only the bars, cafes and China shops (very useful for all Camino needs and momentos) were open so we followed suit and called it a day after 12 paltry kms. We found a picturesque municipal albergue and enjoyed a lovely long picnic next to the river. Lovely until we tried to get up. *Aaarrrggghhh!* pain as muscles we didn't know existed cramped and spasmed and feet muscles went on strike!

Another rule of the Camino: *never be still for long.*

Ribadiso - Palas de Rei

The promise of a peaceful night was interrupted by the usual night time snufflers and snorers, but exacerbated by a wooden floor as the night of the weak bladders and the banging doors dragged on until alarms sounded at 6am.

The sun only rises at 08:45 (mid-October) so it is a case of hurry up and wait as walking the *Camino Regresso* in the dark is not much fun. But the walk was beautiful and Galicia really is paradise! Green meadows, low stone walls, Roman bridges, beautiful churches and the most stunning weather. Another Camino lesson learned - ensure my shoes are tight around my feet before walking downhill. My big toe had a distinct shine to it.

After 23 kms we arrived at Albergue Domingo and were treated to all sorts of surprises including a guest appearance by the Queen of the Camino and her companion, Tigger. An interesting pair indeed who have walked many Caminos!

One's personal space is severely limited when staying in albergues and one needs to get used to all sorts of things including sleeping a foot away from a stranger, a person shaving their face in the senoras' bathroom and understanding the difference between a peregrino menu in Portugal and Spain.

The Portuguese menus were very limited and the helpings quite moderate for a hungry pilgrim. So when we were presented with two different soups, I thought that was it for dinner. I was ravenous so I summoned up courage to brave the kitchen and ask for more kale and bean soup but was greeted with a firm frown. And then I understood why - food flowed from the kitchen including ensalada mixta, green beans and carrots with potatoes and hard boiled eggs and the most delicious meatballs in tomato sauce, two carafes of *vino tinto* and delicious Santiago tarte for dessert.

For some odd reason our host kept bringing me leftovers to finish - apparently he thought I was still hungry. So we rolled into our bunks and prepared for another night of symphonies.

Palas de Rei - Gonza

What a pleasant surprise - not one snorer in the room!

Our *Queen of the Camino* had a brilliant name for our *Camino Regresso* - the *Camino of Smiles* – she said we could smile at our fellow peregrinos instead of studying the contents of their washing hanging on their backpacks.

We walked up and down the picturesque hills of Galicia and visited a beautiful hilltop church, where we lit a candle for Margie. A picnic in a green meadow and 25 kms later we found the smallest albergue with the most beds, the least amount of personal space and the largest number of the loudest snorers. It was going to be a very long night.

Palas de Rei - Sarria

Another early morning eviction which was a relief after a long night of snufflers, snorers, nose trumpeters and coughers. Whew were we glad to be going in the wrong direction and not sharing another albergue with those sick peregrinos. The previous evening we enjoyed another generous peregrino meal except this time I knew to order two starters or I really would tip the bunk bed over as I hoisted myself onto the top bunk. We have now discovered that wooden bunks are preferable to metal bunks. Another lesson learnt on the Camino.

I anticipated a rocky night and to be sure as our Irish friends would say, we felt as if we were on a stormy sea as the occupants of the bunk beds below us battled to get comfortable.

The usual 6am scuffle and wrinkle of plastic bags and *zzzzziiipppp* of sleeping bags and backpacks continued until we were reminded to leave by 8am. The sun only rose just before 9am but it was good to be out early despite a hot berg wind blowing. In the distance we could see the smoky haze of a few wildfires but later they became very serious and some peregrinos had to be evacuated.

Seemed Galicia had also been hit by arsonists.

A long day up and down the dusty paths but the scenery was always breathtakingly beautiful. Another picnic in a meadow and a chance meeting with a young Dane who was insistent that we were walking the wrong way! He was walking the Camino in honour of his late Grandfather and had come armed with everything but the kitchen-sink but included a frying pan.

After nearly 30 kms on the road, we found a beautiful old monastery and respite from the smoke and hot wind.

We met a pilgrim who had moved to Greece and told us very entertaining stories of marrying into an orthodox family. After two bottles of excellent vino tinto and laughing til we cried, Al Greco called it a night. The gods were with us as there were only six peregrinos in the 40-bed room. Only Al Greco snored but he was forgiven for providing priceless entertainment.

Sarria - Triacastela

A sleep-in until 8:30am departure - what a pleasure! Well it could have been but the usual chickens started scratching around at 6am, crowing about their day ahead. The wild fires had worsened through the night and the predicted rain had not arrived.

Sarria was like a ghost town and as we climbed high into the mountains, the air grew darker and smokier and even the birds stopped singing. It was very eerie and we expected nasty zombies to appear from the fog. We somehow lost the yellow arrows walking in reverse and climbed what seemed 2 kms of a near vertical mountain. Summits were great for detoxing and it looked like I had been in a sauna. It is quite tricky deciding what to wear when the weather is iffy as one overheats very quickly carrying a backpack. At the same time one does not want to get drenched or endure a cold wind so wearing a fleece or jacket back to front seemed to be the answer.

A quick picnic of the usual artisan bread, cheese, olives, ham and rooibos tea next to a deserted road and we were off again.

We passed the eco-albergue Al Greco forewarned us about. Apparently pretty girls do yoga poses and stretches and blow kisses to attract the weary peregrinos. But as soon they have them checked in, they are delegated kitchen and garden duties including digging trenches in the veggie garden. All so one can partake in 'ohhhmmmss' at the end of the day.

After summiting Spain's version of Kilimanjaro, we sped past the eco-albergue in search of the Three Castles and a warm shower. We found a lovely albergue next to a river on the outskirts of town where we were serenaded by four snorers and snorters. They sounded just like horses blowing after a race on exhalation. Perhaps they were dreaming of their pacy walk ahead. Oh well, at least my feet got a rest for the night.

Triacastela - O Cebreiro

A long, noisy night but not unusual for the peregrino existence. The weather had changed and drizzle had set in which meant at least we could chose something different to wear from our vast wardrobe. Enter the all encompassing and all covering poncho! It's amazing how little we needed to get by every day as long as we had a little hot water and detergent or shampoo to keep ourselves and our clothes clean.

One usually starts the day full of energy and enthusiasm but it soon becomes just another leg day and the mind and eyes start wandering and looking for entertainment. That day's was how many uses did the locals have for baling twine? A day of ups and downs and watching peregrinos appear out of the mist, until we reached the highest point of the *Camino Francés* some 1,300 odd metres above sea level.

We came across the famous pilgrim statue with a South African flag ribbon tied around his foot and plasters on his massive toes. He reminded us of home and the excellent sense of humour South Africans have, especially when the chips are down.

The Spanish on the other hand have a different sense of humour. They make a Camino path along a main road except the main road is flat and the peregrino path crosses every possible contour. We were quite certain they added a few more ups and downs just to make sure we were totally exhausted by the end of the day.

There is clearly a lot of vandalism along the Camino which is a great pity as most of the churches are locked and barred. The Camino markers have been defaced and the bronze plaques with the distance to Santiago have been removed. I often wondered if the locals were fed up with the thousands of peregrinos who invade their private spaces and country roads.

On the other hand, the entrepreneurs have capitalised on the Camino and opened albergues, pensions, cafes and bars.

It's a hard life especially for those running hospitality venues. There are two or three family members who do everything from cooking, cleaning, preparing beds and mopping up bathrooms, to making hearty dinners and serving the hungry caterpillars. Their children leave for school at around 8:30am and get home around 8pm.

Loud and lively family catch-up time is spent in the restaurants amongst the pilgrims. So different to what we are used to in South Africa but so enjoyable to be part of the lively chats even though we didn't understand a word. We spent a peaceful and warm night in the smallest room of a pension in the hilltop Celtic-like village of O Cebreiro.

O Cebreiro - Trabadelo

A freezing start to the day as we rapidly descended 600m down the slippery, rocky paths while those going the right way had stripped down to t-shirts and were huffing and puffing uphill.

A very enterprising local saddled up his six horses and offered a two-hour ride up the most difficult part of the Camino. We noticed a distinct increase in the number of taxis on the roads and a decrease in the number of peregrinos on the trail. It must have had something to do with that mountain and the rain.

We walked through beautiful little villages and then along busy roads. The Spanish roads are very impressive in the mountainous areas. We found a quaint albergue opposite an ancient church - just in time as another shower of rain came down. For €5.00 each we were very spoilt with pure cotton linen on the bed and a blanket. One usually gets plastic mattress and pillow covers at that price. Our hostess couldn't be more friendly and gave us all a warm hug good night.

Trabadelo – Ponferrada

Exactly three weeks on the road and we had covered about 450 kms. It didn't seem that impressive until we looked at the tread left on our shoes or how many rubber stoppers we had used on our walking poles. Our backpacks seemed lighter and our bodies fitter but our feet still questioned what they had done to deserve such punishment.

A varied and overcast day of walking along main roads, through deserted villages and then the scenic vineyards of Bierzo. A beautiful sight as the vines and poplars were changing colour.

A slight wrong turn when we ran out of yellow arrows in reverse, cost us an hour but we saw a beautiful suburb which assured us that parts of Spain were alive and thriving.

A long walk through two light industrial areas and we eventually ran out of steam at 8pm. We were still off the Camino track but settled for a night in a hotel in the heart of local land where the 10pm curfew/lights out that we valued so much was the 10pm wake up for the locals. Earplugs and eye masks are a must on the Camino and that night was no exception.

Ponferrada - Riego de Ambros

A long walk out of a big city and then we understood why the Camino entered from the west. It is far more scenic with lovely historical buildings while the east is a light industrial and motor town and enough to make one catch a bus out.

The long walk back into the countryside continued until we hit the steep ascent into the mountains at Molinaseca where the plane trees are pruned in a very unique way.

After watching a young man hobbling down the hill with a knee guard (he had taken a tumble in the shale) we kept to the main road and avoided the dangerous Camino path.

The spectacular countryside reminded us so much of South Africa and the Eastern Cape. A tough day and eventually a night in a cupboard albergue where the bunk beds were screened off from each other with sliding doors – very ingenious indeed.

Our wonderful, warm hostess, Isa made us feel very welcome and she loved practicing our names. Her eyes lit up when she saw Robin's passport - 'Ahhh Robbeeen Hood!' After a dinner fit for more than two ravenous peregrinos, overlooking a quaint church and a sunset to remember, we had a peaceful night in our cupboard, simply content with a few aches and pains.

Riego de Ambros - El Ganso

THE WORST DAY! A cold front had passed through during the night and an icy wind blew. The warm sun of Portugal seemed a distant memory and another long, long day ascending 600 m up a windy road.

The Camino track tempted us as it seemed more direct than the main road but we could see the undulating path it followed. A couple of local dogs kept us company but when the road intersected the Camino path, they happily bounced after peregrinos heading back into their village. The road ascended on and on, up the mountain in the icy wind and our feet ached. We'd both picked up the lurgy from the smallest albergue with the least personal space and the most sick people and were not feeling too clever.

Why were we doing this to ourselves?

Family and friends and home comforts filled our thoughts and conversation and, in desperation we started playing I Spy. I realised things were really bad when I couldn't even guess T for Tree.

We passed a tiny deserted enclave where Thomas from Ponferrada decided he had received a templar calling and runs a refugio. It must be one of the most unique and basic albergues and there is the added bonus of an adrenaline rush if one needs the bathroom during the night. The Letrina is across the main road balancing on a rocky outcrop.

The Camino always provides - eventually - but only once one has been thoroughly challenged and nearly on one's knees. In this case we found the quaintest medieval restaurant in Foncebadon and felt we were in another a time period and awaited for the knights to arrive.

Pumpkin soup warmed the soul and sick and deer stew filled the recovering. We felt revived and back on track. But all too soon every footstep felt like we were walking on thorns, our backpacks felt full of rocks and I just wanted my mum!.

The road went on and on and I tried to remember the words of the highwayman and the gusty galleon and the ribbon road in the moonlight and Beth the landlord's black eyed daughter until the highwayman went down like a dog but I just couldn't remember the correct version.

So we tried the pilgrim path with pebbles and rocks to distract ourselves. *I Spy, General Knowledge* and any game we could think of frustrated us more than helped us. It was our worst day so far. And then we found another tiny village - El Ganso and a welcoming fire in a cosy albergue, Marie (in this case Maria) biscuits, hot chocolate, warm duvets and a lovely couple from Lithuania. I could manage one more night without my mum.

El Gonso - Hospital de Orbigo

An icy start as frost lay all around and we considered checking back into the cosy albergue with the warm fire. But we had places to go, a cafe grande con leche was awaiting and we had heard about the delicious pastries at Astorga. A young man with blue hair stopped and talked excitedly about our *Camino Regresso* and placed strings with brightly coloured plastic hands around our necks. We didn't understand a word but decided the hands were there to carry us through rough days. Good timing after two days of solid climbing!

The scenery changed again and the dry, dusty and feet murdering pebbles paths led us east.

A stop in Astorga at the most beautiful cathedral, Gaudi's museum and a mandatory stop at Alfonso's for their famous pastries and chocolate kept us going. Sunday is family day in Spain and the squares and sidewalks were filled with the energy of family and friends and loud chatter and laughter. The shops closed by 12pm and only cafes, bars and restaurants remained open.

The locals certainly have their priorities right.

We plodded on up and down the pebbled hills until we came across another pilgrim who had received his calling. David opened the *House of Desires* from an abandoned barn and offered free fruit and juices to a hammock or an outside bed to rest the weary bones. What a saint!

Sunday is also hunting day - big men in camo with big guns and excited dogs! Although we are not sure what they hunt as there is not much sign of wildlife apart from the road signs with deer. We heard the shots around us as we plodded on through the farm lands flanked by oak forests and were convinced the hunters in the forests knew pilgrims were out on a Sunday too.

But I was very wrong - suddenly dogs dashed out of the forest in front of me and dust shot up as bullets sprayed around the dogs. It was a wonder the dogs didn't get a bullet, never mind two exhausted pilgrims!

I did a bit of fancy foot dance despite the pain and five big men appeared with guns slung over their shoulders. That was a close shave!

Another two hours of painful feet and aching muscles, but determined to keep our sense of humour in check, we reached Obrigo. A little medicinal wine and beer to ease the pain and we learnt how to count in Spanish as the locals enjoyed bingo night. The end was in sight and it had been a fabulous journey with amazing experiences and interesting people from all over the world. There was so much to reflect on and so much to appreciate. Like my own bed and a car for a start.

Obrigo

Somewhere just outside Leon - the unattractive part of the French Camino. We had walked nearly 600 kms or possibly more and it certainly felt that way.

A lunch stop where we learned the plastic hands we were given were to spread awareness of childhood cancer. How appropriate as my son had overcome his battle of childhood leukaemia. Walking along the main road was too noisy to reflect or even talk to each other so it was a silent walk in noise pollution and pain.

The previous day, I proved stretching is very bad for one especially once one is warmed up.

First major injury of the Camino just before the finish line! It felt like a strained muscle or ligament or something with lots of nerve endings that felt like a 6 inch nail through my leg? I tried walking skew, turning my foot in or out or walking on my toes but nothing helped. A *Transact* patch and a bandage were not going to save the day.

What was the Camino trying to provide for me today? To accept help? To know it's OK to lean on someone? To hand over my backpack and ease the pain?

And were the tears of pain or frustration? Did we call it a day and catch a taxi to Leon or keep on hobbling and hope that my pride would heal my pain? A few Spanish gates distracted me for a while, a cup of rooibos at a bus stop and just when the journey became overwhelming, a surprise awaited - a brand new albergue with a little oasis behind the big walls next to the noisy road in the arid, barren flatlands.

For the first time on the Camino I was too tired to do the chores. I had a clean shirt for the morning and a bed for the night. The rest could take care of itself as long as I could walk again in the morning.

Valverde de Virgen - Leon

A half day covering only 12.5 kms but the weather was very pleasant for late October. We had a quick cup of tea with new friends who very discreetly told me they were both in the medical field. They diagnosed my shin splint and said I should not be walking at all! So we waited until they had disappeared over the rise, and I started walking - very slowly.

A very pleasant toddle into Leon, a picnic and a siesta in a city park and then into the old centre of Leon, past magnificent buildings and the Cathedral of Leon dedicated to Santa Maria. As we were looking for a place to stay, a friendly nun herded us into the municipal albergue run by her church but the lack of personal space and thought of another night of symphonies in such close proximity, kept us moving on. We must have looked a sight, limping around and looking quite battered when a peregrino invited us to stay in their *AirBnB* apartment. Despite the shower being the size of two placemats, we were ecstatic about the change of accommodation.

We shared an exceptionally fun evening with eight new friends, hearing their adventures (including two Camino love stories), their ups and downs and war wounds and so much more.

People really share a lot on the Camino - I guess they feel it is a safe space to be themselves. Delicious salads and pizzas accompanied by some yellow poison - medicinal apparently and especially for sore feet, blisters and shin splints. Close to midnight (no albergue curfew thank goodness!), we somehow climbed the eight flights of stairs to what we thought was our private penthouse. As we closed our eyes for a peaceful night, the door creaked open and we had company.

A young couple with a distressed baby had booked into the spare room for the night. The Camino certainly provides but also tests one's sense of humour! Earplugs and an extra pillow over the head but we were so exhausted, the crying baby serenaded us to sleep.

At least we had the following day off in Leon.

Leon

We had covered 650-odd kilometres and had a kaleidoscope of memories and experiences to take home.

The most challenging part would be to return to normality after our nomadic existence with hardly a care in the world.

It felt very odd walking around Leon without our backpacks and we missed having everything we needed on our back. The main plaza had transformed into a feast for the eyes with a fresh fruit and veggie market and mobile vans filled with jamon, chorizo, cecina, bacalau and queso lined the street. The vendors are incredibly generous, offering tastings of all their products, and not expecting any purchases in return. But the hungry caterpillar and his rubber arm accomplice could not resist so we purchased a few goodies for breakfast number two.

The Leon Cathedral is a beautiful and imposing building and as we had not visited one church on the Camino (they are all locked due to vandalism), we could not miss this opportunity. A very informative narrative about the history of the cathedral, the architectural design, it's near ruin and subsequent revamp left me in awe of the passion of the residents of Leon from around 1300 until the present day.

The detail on the expansive stain glass windows and the thought that went into what details should appear on which side according to the angle of the sun was just a small part of this masterpiece.

It's amazing how exhausted one gets when one does not have a purpose such as walking 25-30 kms. So we decided to walk to the bus station and buy our tickets to Burgos.

As the machine printed out our tickets it struck me that this really was the end. No more albergues, no more squeaky bunk beds and rustling sleeping bags, no more meadow picnics, no more snorers, sleep talkers, early morning alarms and scuffling in plastic bags, no more washing clothes and drying them on our backpacks, no more pilgrim meals and stamps in our passports, no hola and buen camino greetings as we walked regresso.

I would miss everything!

Our *Camino of Smiles* and four weeks of carefree days had come to an end. They always say it's best to leave on a high but I could not have felt more down. Could we not postpone our flights and walk to Burgos? And while we're at it, Logroño, and oh well, let's walk to Madrid? But sense prevailed and we decided we would be back soon to experience a different route.

A sundowner on the benches outside the Cathedral turned into a fun filled evening as interesting conversations of why we were all walking the Camino flowed with vino verano, chips, pizza and ice cream - classic pilgrim food when one is exhausted. Our Italian football friend kept the supply of San Miguels flowing and was determined to celebrate this special moment for one simple reason - *'Eeet eeesa the Cameeeno!'*

At least we ended our amazing adventure with a night (and a view) to remember!

Buen Camino, til next time

About Sarah Hewitt Rippon

Sarah Hewitt Rippon is an equine experiential facilitator living in Cape Town, South Africa. She took six weeks off in September/October 2017 to walk the Portuguese Camino and celebrate her 50th birthday.

On reaching Santiago, she headed east to Leon, walking part of the French Camino in reverse. *The Camino of Smiles* provided endless insights and entertainment to her own life as well as that of fellow pilgrims which were recorded in lighthearted daily anecdotes, photographs and videos.

The experience proved life-changing as she had to overcome various challenges and sensitivities. Sarah returned to South Africa and is planning to walk another Camino, be it in Spain or elsewhere around the world.

https://www.linkedin.com/in/sarah-hewitt-b8298614

The Zero Point Field

Simon Welsh

Just outside of space-time is a place you've always been,
Though it may be that you cannot well remember what you've seen.
All of who you are is there – not just ten per cent.
The real you is quantum. You vibrate with pure intent;

A frequency of light and sound, directed here and there.
You don't exist at all and yet you're always everywhere.
The moment's all there is and can't be measured on a line.
There is no right or wrong because the moment is divine.

You are the creator of the frequency of youth:
Born in swirling symphonies of nothing but the Truth.
Age cannot affect you for the only moment's now.
And your mission is delightful – to explore yourself. But how?

As Truth, you are the answer to the question with no name.
The journey lasts forever and it's nothing but a game.
So when you last decided that you'd like to come to Earth,
That you wanted to explore human beingness from birth.

You knew what you were doing. Your choice to come was true.
You manifested simply in the frequency of You.
But somewhere you forgot the truth; let it fall away;
You forgot this was a game; that your mission is to play.

But now you are remembering that Truth is who you are;
That you are not your body, nor your thoughts about your car,
Nor your marriage nor your misery; your spectrum of emotion;
You are just a drop of water looking for the ocean.

But here's the thing – a drop of water falling from the sky.
Does not attempt to take control – it does not try to fly.
A drop of water gives itself to gravity and peace,
And when it hits the ocean . . . it's the ultimate release.

We are like those drops of water, falling from the sky.
But we do not surrender. We resist. And here's why:
We're scared of life. We scared of Death. We're scared of being bold.
We're scared of one another, and we're scared of growing old.

We're scared that if we join this ocean, we will disappear.
We're scared of what will happen if we give in to that fear.
But just the other side of fear, whispering and true,
Is the zero point, our place of birth, calling me and you.

So when we let our conscious thoughts descend like drops of rain,
They will sink into the heart and join the ocean with no name.
And there, together, consciously, as many and as One,
The zero point will shine through us as brightly as the Sun.

Would You Like To Share Your Camino Story in *My Camino Walk #2*?

We are now collating more stories for *My Camino Walk #2* which will coincide with a late Summer-early Autumn global *Amazon* paperback and *Kindle* release.

Here's how it works.

Basically, you provide us with a first-person, personal story - *by you* - around 1,500 words, that shares your Camino journey, your insights, your tips and your experience.

We also need a third-person 200 word bio - *about you* - your internet links and a high res JPEG headshot (600kb+).

Interested? Please email *coachbiz@hotmail.com* and we will send you the full *My Camino Walk Writers Guide*.